Are you gl

One in ten people are **gluten**
Do you or your family have any

- [ ] tired and exhausted
- [ ] bloating or gas troubles
- [ ] gastric reflux or heartburn

- [ ] ...comfortable tummy
- [ ] diarrhoea/constipation

- [ ] not growing well
- [ ] lack of energy
- [ ] unhappy with your weight

- [ ] eating problems
- [ ] weakness

- [ ] chronic iron deficiency
- [ ] runny nose and sinus problems
- [ ] osteoporosis, bone and joint pains

- [ ] headaches or migraine
- [ ] hard to think clearly
- [ ] dermatitis, eczema or bad skin

- [ ] depressed or moody
- [ ] poor sleep

- [ ] hyperactive or cranky
- [ ] mental health problems
- [ ] Attention Deficit Hyperactivity Disorder (ADHD)

- [ ] autism

If you can answer "yes" to some of these problems, then you, or your child, has a high chance of being **gluten-sensitive**.

Your questions answered

This book gives you answers the questions that I am so frequently asked about gluten. It gives you the "who", "what" and "why" of gluten reactions. If you are gluten-sensitive, then you will at last feel great and full of energy again. Let's get started!

DoctorGluten ®

1

Are You Gluten-Sensitive?
Your questions answered.

Copyright 2006 RRS Global Ltd.
Author: Dr Rodney Ford

National Library of New Zealand Cataloguing-in-Publication Data
Ford, Rodney, 1949-
Are you gluten-sensitive? : your questions answered /
Rodney Ford.
Previous ed.: 2005.
ISBN-13: 978-0-473-11229-5
ISBN-10: 0-473-11229-9
1. Food allergy—Diet therapy—Popular works. 2. Gluten-free
diet— Recipes. 3. Nutrition—Popular works. I. Title.
641.56318—dc 22

Published by RRS Global Ltd.
PO Box 25-360, Christchurch, New Zealand
www.doctorgluten.com
Printed by Tien Wah Press, Singapore
Third Edition

Jacket cover, art work and illustrations
by Liz Fazakarley of *Ford Design*.
Recipes collated by Chris Ford.

2

Dedication

To all the beautiful children

and wonderful parents

who have taught us so much.

Disclaimer

The contents of this book are Dr Rodney Ford's own personal viewpoint of the gluten-sensitive problem, based on the data he has analyzed from his patients.

Every effort has been taken to ensure that the recipes in this book are correct. As these recipes have been contributed, we cannot be held responsible for the results or for infringement of any copyrights. If you see your recipe in this book, we thank you in advance.

We hope that this book and these recipes will help you with your gluten-free diet.

Contents

About the author

Dr Rodney Ford
Professor
MB BS MD FRACP MCCCH ASM

Dr Rodney Ford is a Paediatric Gastroenterologist, Nutrition Consultant and an Allergist. He has been Associate Professor of Paediatrics at the Christchurch School of Medicine, University of Otago, New Zealand. He has an international reputation.

He has been investigating and managing people with nutrition and food problems for more than twenty years. In that time there have been huge changes on the perspective of coeliac disease. More importantly, there has been a big change in thinking about the problem of accurately identifying people who are gluten-sensitive.

Rodney has spent his career trying to understand how some foods can make you feel so unwell. Every day he sees children and adults who, unknowingly, suffer from symptoms caused by their food. He wants people to understand how food works so that they can live healthier and longer lives. He sees so many people who eat the wrong types of food because of their lack of understanding of how food works in their body.

Rodney graduated with Honours from the University of New South Wales in 1974 (M.B. B.S.). He went on to study food allergy, food intolerance and gastroenterology in New Zealand, in Australia and in the United Kingdom. He qualified as Fellow of the Royal Australasian College of Physicians in Paediatrics (F.R.A.C.P.) in 1981. He was awarded his Doctorate of Medicine (M.D.) by the University of New South Wales in 1982 with his thesis "Food hypersensitivity in children: diagnostic approaches to milk and egg hypersensitivity."

He runs a busy private allergy, gastroenterology and nutrition clinic. He has written over a hundred and twenty scientific papers, including books and book chapters. He has been involved in ground-breaking work in the areas of Sudden Infant Death Syndrome (SIDS), breastfeeding, caffeine exposure, food allergy and gluten-sensitivity.

He keenly wants you to understand about gluten-sensitivity and its multiplicity of symptoms. He presents you the data which backs up his opinion on the diagnosis and management of those who are gluten-sensitive. He has a new approach to the diagnosis and management of gluten-sensitivity.

This book is the first in a series of six books on gluten which puts forward his views on this huge problem and then gives you lots of information and recipes to help you along on your gluten-free journey:
o   Are You Gluten-Sensitive? Your Questions Answered.
o   The Book for the Sick, Tired and Grumpy.
o   Full of it! The shocking truth about gluten
     (The brain-grain connection).
o   Going Gluten-Free: How to Get Started.
o   The Gluten-Free Lunch Book.
o   Gluten-Free Parties and Picnics.

He hopes that this information will benefit you and hundreds of thousands of others, worldwide.

Your questions answered

Did you answer "yes" to any of the gluten questions on the front page? If so, then you might want to read this book. Questions usually provoke even more questions. But good answers can be hard to get because knowledge is on the move. What seemed right yesterday can be wrong tomorrow. The area of gluten-sensitivity is no exception. It is controversial.

Over the last fifty years the understanding of the nature of gluten toxicity has rapidly evolved. As new information emerges, our thinking must subsequently change. This has led to confusion everywhere about the diagnosis and management of people who are gluten-sensitive. The purpose of this book is to clarify this muddle.

Coeliac disease is now recognised to be very common, affecting about one in a hundred people. However, only a small proportion of these people have been diagnosed. Therefore, there are yet vast numbers who still remain undiagnosed and who have significant health problems.

Gluten-sensitivity has gone virtually unnoticed

Now multiply this problem ten times! My data shows that this is the size of the gluten-sensitivity problem. It is ten times more common that coeliac disease, but this condition has been largely ignored by the medical profession. Bad health caused by gluten is just starting to be recognised as a huge health crisis. Are you part of it? Are you affected by gluten?

Gluten is causing a health crisis

This book discusses the issues surrounding the new knowledge about gluten-sensitivity and how it differs from coeliac disease.

The structure of this book is based on the questions that I am repeatedly asked. I have answered all of these questions in detail and put them into the clinical context. There is a rapid unfolding of knowledge. There is still a great deal more to find out. Therefore, some answers remain incomplete.

The questions that I am asked indicate the uncertainty and misunderstandings that so many people have about gluten and how it can lead to poor health and disease. Many others have never heard about gluten and the harm it can do.

The questions fall into these ten broad categories which I have used for chapter headings:

1 What does gluten do to my gut?
2 Do I have gluten-sensitivity or coeliac disease?
3 What symptoms can be caused by gluten?
4 Do I need a small bowel biopsy?
5 What blood tests should I have and why?
6 How long does gluten-sensitivity last – is it lifelong?
7 What is a gluten-free diet – how can I do that?
8 Can you convince me with your gluten-sensitive data?
9 What are your hints on going gluten-free?
10 Do you have any good gluten-free recipes for me?

The following chapters contain my answers. My opinion has been formed by my extensive dealings with gluten-sensitive children and adults, and from researching up-to-date medical literature. There is some repetition to ensure that the answers to each question are mostly complete. This is not a text book and I have chosen not to include the medical journal references. I welcome feedback from you. Please send me your questions to answer. I thank all of the children and parents who have enlightened me about the problems and solutions to gluten.

1. What does gluten do to my gut?

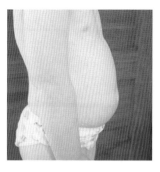

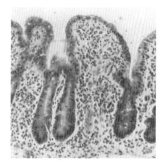

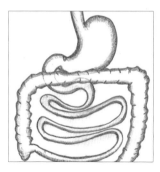

What happens in my gut?

Have you ever thought of yourself as a long tube with arms and legs? Well, that might be how a gastroenterologist might see you. The names used to denote your "gut" include the "gastro-intestinal tract", "intestinal tract", "intestines" and "bowel". These terms are often used interchangeably.

To understand what gluten does, it is first necessary to learn about how your gut works. So, let's go down this tube. Use the diagram for your guide.

Your gastro-intestinal "tube" starts at your teeth and mouth (chewing), and then to your oesophagus (swallowing). This chewing starts off the digestive process with the saliva in your mouth breaking down sugars with the enzyme "amylase".

You are a long tube

Your stomach then grinds and mixes the food with more enzymes and acid. The acid is produced in the stomach primarily to kill the bugs that are in your food to stop them from invading you: the acid is a barrier to bugs.

Your stomach empties the ground-up food, bit by bit, into your small intestine (where food gets absorbed). This is the digestive part of your gut where the food gets broken down into its component parts. Only then can it be absorbed. If this system malfunctions, then you cannot extract the goodness of your food – this is the cause of "mal-absorption" (literally, bad absorption). When this occurs, the food goodness passes right through you. You can lose fats, proteins, sugars, minerals and vitamins this way. This can cause diarrhoea in some people.

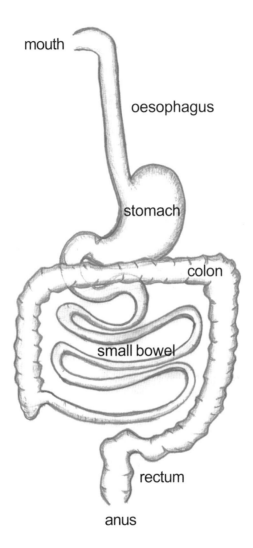

The large bowel (also called the colon) is the last section of your gut. Here you process the waste material – faeces or "poos". The proper functioning of your colon is critical for you to feel comfortable.

Your colon is teeming with bacteria (bugs) that process the fibre in your diet. The right fibre and the right bugs in your colon are essential for your good health and your immune function. Finally, your bowel motions are stored in the rectum and expelled through the anus.

So yes, your gut is a long tube that sequentially processes your food. Each part is important. This gut mechanism is absolutely essential to keep you alive and well. Everything that you put in your mouth eventually gets processed and it is either absorbed or excreted.

Your good health relies on the health of your gut

The only control that you have on your body, from the point of view of food, is to decide what you put into your mouth. Once you have swallowed it and this food is in your stomach, then your physiology takes over.

If you are mal-absorbing your food, then more fat passes straight through you. Lots of fat in the faeces makes it pale and smelly. This fat will also cause your faeces to float in the toilet pan. This type of stool is called steatorrhoea.

Many of the problems that you can develop with coeliac disease are because of this malabsorption.

This malabsorption is what makes your faeces abnormal. This malabsorption also robs you of your much-needed nutrients.

Where does gluten do its damage?

Gluten can play havoc everywhere in your gut. It also can affect you in many of your other organs. If you are sensitive to gluten, then your elegant gut mechanism can be disrupted in many places. This is the basis of the host of possible symptoms.

Gluten can cause havoc everywhere

Every part of your gastro-intestinal tract (your gut) can be affected – not only the small bowel, but also your mouth, oesophagus, stomach, small bowel and colon. I call these the target organs.

In addition, there are other target organs in your body, outside of your gut, that can be directly involved. These are your brain, joints, skin and your immune system.

On top of all of this, with the poor assimilation of foods and minerals, all of the symptoms of nutritional deficiency (from malabsorption) can appear (anaemia, iron deficiency, tiredness, osteoporosis, low immune function, weak muscles and nerve damage).

Tiredness and exhaustion are common

We will deal more with these symptoms later. Perhaps the most frequent symptom is a feeling of tiredness and exhaustion. This can come on gradually, so that it can be hard to recognise. This exhaustion can be put down to all of the things that you do in your busy life. But some busy people do not get tired!

If you have had long-standing symptoms of any description, then you might be gluten-sensitive. You need to be tested.

What is gluten?

Gluten is the central character in this book. Gluten is a protein. It is found in the cereals: wheat, rye and barley. Very small amounts, of similar protein fragments (avenin) are also found in oats. Gluten and its relationship to oats is a contentious issue.

Gluten is a natural part of the proteins of these grains. It gets its name gluten because, when cooked, it goes sticky like glue. Gluten is the stuff that makes bread dough sticky, such that it won't easily come off your hands.

Gluten glues foods together

However, gluten is very useful in cooking and baking. Gluten helps to stick food components together. When you make bread and muffins, and all your wonderful baking, it is this gluten that glues the food ingredients together. It traps the air so that you can make airy, fluffy, light food. Gluten prevents your baking from falling apart into a heap of crumbs.

Once you take the gluten out of the food, you get much smaller air pockets in the baking. That is why gluten-free baking can be rather firm and solid. That is the technical problem of taking gluten out of your diet.

It is an irritating fact that gluten is found in the three cereals wheat, rye and barley.

More about oats later. But briefly, the evidence is that most people who are gluten-sensitive can safely eat moderate amounts of oats. Each person needs to assess their own approach to oats by trial and error.

What is the difference between gluten and gliadin?

Technically, gluten is the protein that is left behind after all the starch is washed away from wheat flour. However, gluten is actually made up of two main groups of proteins: the gliadins and the glutenins.

When these gluten proteins are digested, they are broken down into much smaller pieces (these are called peptide chains). Several of these peptide chains are harmful to those who are gluten-sensitive or who are coeliacs. These peptides can cause damage when they are put directly into the small intestine. An unusual feature of these gluten peptides is that they are relatively resistant to digestion in your gut.

There are similar peptide chains in wheat, rye and barley. However, the oat proteins have slightly different peptide chains – so these *may not* be harmful to coeliac patients or to those with a gluten-sensitivity.

When we talk about a "gluten-free" diet, we are actually talking about our food being completely free of these harmful peptides from wheat, barley, rye and (possibly but probably not) oats.

Gluten comes from wheat, barley and rye

Where is gluten found?

Substantial gluten is a protein found in these three grains:
- o   wheat
- o   barley
- o   rye

So all foods made with *any* of these grains will contain gluten (unless they are very specially processed to completely extract the gluten).

The good news is that gluten is *not* found in rice and corn. The bad news is that gluten is a useful protein in the manufacturing and processing of many foods.

Also, the starches that are found in grains are a common food ingredient. This grain-starch can be made from wheat. Therefore, many processed foods (that is anything in a packet or in a can) may contain gluten. Beware of any food in a packet.

Individual sensitivity to gluten is extremely varied

Some people are extraordinarily sensitive to gluten. Even the tiniest bit of gluten makes them feel unwell. In these individuals, oats sometimes causes them gut symptoms as well. It is important to emphasise that any oats that are eaten must be free of any other contaminating cereals.

To add to the confusion, many people can eat small amounts of gluten and get no symptoms, whatsoever. However, the gluten (in those without symptoms) can still cause them substantial gut damage.

The philosophy of food labelling has also changed. Tiny traces of gluten in foods were previously not recorded on food labels. However, new rules on food labelling have reduced the official "tolerance" to gluten. This means that foods, once deemed gluten-free, are now regarded as containing gluten.

Individual sensitivity to gluten is extremely varied

There are varying degrees of sensitivity to gluten. Also, people find that their own gluten tolerance changes as the years go by. Those people who do not get any symptoms when they eat gluten can usually take oats without a problem.

However, the question remains "Are there enough gluten-like peptides in oats to give subtle changes in the gut in a few individuals?"

Is gluten found in oats?

There has been controversy for years as to whether it is okay, or not okay, to eat oats if you are gluten-sensitive.

Several recent clinical studies have now provided very good evidence that oats do *not* damage the gut mucosa in most people who have coeliac disease. Following this, guidelines from some Coeliac Societies now accept that moderate amounts of oats *can* be consumed by most coeliacs without risk.

Many experts concerned with coeliac disease have now concluded that oats are *safe* for coeliacs, as long as they limit their consumption to amounts "found to be safe" in these research studies.

This *safe* quantity is up to one-half cup of dry whole-grain rolled oats per day. Please note that any oats that are consumed need to be free of any contamination from other grains.

Half a cup of oats each day is usually okay

Here is some of the information that this opinion is based on:

A study in Finland looked at 52 coeliacs who were in remission and who had been on a gluten-free diet for more than a year. They all had a duodenal-biopsy, then they ate about 50 grams of oats (half a cup) per day over the next six months. Finally, they had a second biopsy. None of the people had any villus damage (more about small bowel biopsy in Chapter 4).

Your gut can heal whilst eating oats

Another group studied 40 newly diagnosed coeliacs in the same way. As expected, their initial biopsy showed significant villus damage (this was because they were still on a gluten-containing diet until they began the study). These people started on their gluten-free diet as well as eating their 50 grams of oats each day for 12 months. At the end of the year, their biopsies showed no damage to their villi. The meaning of this study was that their damaged villi were able to heal while eating oats.

A few people get unwell eating oats

However, other studies have found that not all people with coeliac disease are able to tolerate oats. Especially, those who also have dermatitis herpetiformis. Researchers report that although oats are well tolerated by most coeliacs, they did find a few exceptions. Several people recounted initial abdominal discomfort and bloating. A few patients have been found to eventually develop total villous atrophy during an oat challenge.

Yet another study has investigated 20 adult coeliacs who were in remission, to see if they could eat even larger amounts of oats in their daily gluten-free diet. They consumed about 100 grams (one cup) of uncontaminated rolled oats in their daily diet for over a year. They were tested four times during the study period. This included small bowel endoscopy and blood samples. They experienced no gut symptoms. Also, there were no adverse effects seen in small bowel histology or in their blood test results. The conclusion was that the vast majority of adults with coeliac disease could include large amounts of rolled oats in their diet without problems.

Oats have also been studied in children. A group of ten children with coeliac disease were investigated at the time of their diagnosis. They were put on a gluten-free diet but they were also eating about 25 grams (quarter of a cup) of rolled oats each day. After six months they were tested again. There was improvement in both their small bowel histology and their tissue transglutaminase antibody results (these blood tests are discussed in Chapter 5).

Children tolerate oats well

However, there is still a word of caution. Oat proteins have been shown to trigger the immune response of cells taken from coeliac people. Therefore, the long-term effects of oat cereal added to a gluten-free diet in children still need to be determined.

Oats are useful fibre

The ability to use oats in your diet gives an important source of fibre as well as other important nutrients. This is very important in children who have other food allergies. If you are also allergic to cow's milk and eggs, then going gluten-free is a big task. Therefore, if oats can be tolerated, this makes food planning just a little bit easier.

Each person will have to work out whether or not they can tolerate oats for themselves. This needs to be determined both clinically and with follow-up blood tests.

Testing for oats is trial and error

Finally, other gluten experts have expressed some further concerns about oats. These are:

o   Some food chemistry research studies suggest that avenin protein in oats does have toxic properties.

o   The purity of oat products in some countries is suspect. Oats and oat products can inadvertently be contaminated with wheat. This can occur during harvesting, milling and processing.

o   There is a possibility that gut damage from oats takes longer than six to twelve months to show up. Also, symptoms might not be readily apparent to the person.

o   The possibility that young children might have a higher cross-sensitivity to oats because of their relatively immature immune system.

These are real concerns. It is important that gluten-sensitive people know about the oats story. Whether or not they choose to eat oats, they should be under some sort of regular medical evaluation and supervision.

Know your oats

2. Is it gluten-sensitivity or coeliac disease?

The changing understanding of gluten-sensitivity

Coeliac disease has a long history. However, diagnosing people as being gluten-sensitive is a relatively new concept. The purpose of this book is to describe these two entities side-by-side so that the differences and similarities can be seen. They are both valid diagnoses.

120 years ago

When you understand the history, then you can understand the confusion. Cast your mind back to over 100 years ago. The entity of "coeliac disease" was first described by Samuel Gee in 1888. He called it "the Coeliac affection".

Gee had recognized a group of people, particularly children between one and five years old, who had smelly pale bowel motions, who did not look at all well, who had a pot belly, who were fatigued and who did not grow well.

He did not know what caused this disease. But he did recognise this as a clinical pattern of what is called "malabsorption". These people had a severe nutritional deficiency and did not live very long.

Coeliac disease was a gut disease

Thus, coeliac disease had been defined as a malabsorption condition.

The story of coeliac disease began 120 years ago. The time-line of the history of the understanding of coeliac disease is shown in the Table. Each row is equivalent to 10 years – a decade. As you can see, not much more happened for the next 50 years.

Milestones of coeliac disease/ gluten-sensitivity

Decade	Significant Event
1890	Samuel Gee – "Coeliac Affection"
1900	-
1910	-
1920	-
1930	-
1940	-
1950	Gluten toxicity recognised
1960	Villus atrophy demonstrated
1970	Small bowel biopsy mandatory for diagnosis
1980	First blood tests – anti-reticulin antibodies
1990	Blood tests become widely available
2000	Tissue Transglutaminase (tTG) introduced
2010	Gluten-sensitivity universally recognised?

Each row of the table is equivalent to 10 years.

Gluten discovered as the problem

It was not until 1950 (less than 60 years ago) that Willem Dicke recognised that this "affection" was a disease caused by the toxic effects of eating gluten. He observed that when these patients were taken off wheat, they quickly recovered. With this breakthrough, the pace of understanding quickened.

Abnormal gut tissue found

Seven years later, in 1957, Dr Margo Shiner, a Paediatric Gastroenterologist, was the first person to obtain a piece of tissue from the small intestine from a child who had been diagnosed clinically as having coeliac disease.

Under the microscope, she found that the skin (mucosa) of the intestine was very abnormal – this appearance was called "villus atrophy". This is the description of the flattened appearance of the bowel lining due to the gluten damage.

25

This was the stimulus to find indirect ways of measuring malabsorption. The xylose absorption test was perhaps the most widely adopted test.

Advent of the small bowel biopsy
In the 1960s, the next step was to develop the technique to obtain these small pieces of bowel tissue for examination. This procedure is called a "small bowel biopsy". Initially, it was performed by swallowing a special tiny steel capsule on the end of a long thin tube (the Crosby capsule).

Coeliac disease was small bowel damage

Nowadays, this biopsy tissue is obtained by flexible endoscopy (under a light anaesthetic in children).

The coming of blood tests
Nearly 20 years later, the first blood tests were being investigated to look for coeliac disease. I then had a position as Fellow in Gastroenterology in London, at the Queen Elizabeth Hospital for Children where these new tests were being evaluated. This first test was the Reticulum Antibody test. This was a tissue antibody test that indicated that there was a degree of tissue damage going on. It was not a very sensitive test but it was useful start.

About five years later, in 1985, these blood tests started being done throughout the world.

A big leap forward came when the measurements of IgG-gliadin and IgA-gliadin antibodies were developed (these are also called anti-gliadin antibodies). These tests revealed the degree to which the person's immune system was reacting against gluten.

After yet another 10 years the more specific Endomesial Antibody (EMA) tests were introduced and these have been found to be the most sensitive antibodies so far for the screening of populations. This is a tissue damage test. It tells you if there is any small bowel damage from gluten.

Finally, tissue Transglutaminase (tTG) antibodies were discovered. These are the most specific antibodies for the diagnosis of classical coeliac disease. In other words, there is a high correlation between high tTG antibody levels and an abnormal small bowel biopsy.

Gluten-sensitivity is more than coeliac disease

Gluten-sensitivity is much more than a gut disease
But the biggest step forward has been the realisation that the harm from gluten is much more widespread than just the gut damage of coeliac disease. Most recently, there has been a widening understanding of the effects of gluten-sensitivity *outside* the gastro-intestinal tract.

Both children and adults can have adverse reactions to gluten *without* having observable tissue changes in the small bowel. However, they do have raised gluten antibody levels. Although coeliac disease has mainly been viewed as a gastroenterological condition, gluten-sensitivity needs be seen in a bigger context.

Who is up to date?
When, and from whom, did you get your knowledge about coeliac disease? If you were doing your medical training in the year before Gee, then you would never have heard of coeliac disease! If you did your medical training in 1950, and you did not catch up, you would never have known about the bad effects of gluten.

You need to be current in your knowledge because the concept of gluten-sensitivity is rapidly changing. The most recent information is to do with the area of gluten-sensitivity rather than established coeliac disease. I have estimated that bad reactions to gluten are experience by one in ten people. The problem of gluten-sensitivity is enormous.

The sequence effect
To understand changing knowledge, it is helpful to understand the sequence effect.

You experience each day as it comes, one at a time: day after day. Each day comes in a sequence, one after the other.

Information and knowledge also comes as a sequence. Something is discovered, a tool is created, an idea is generated. The actual sequence of these discoveries and experiences has a big influence on people's thinking.

To date, there has been a hundred years of thinking that coeliac disease is only a gut disease. So, when the blood tests became available, people could only think about the damage to the gut.

However, if the blood tests had been developed first, then the whole area of gluten-sensitivity would have a different perspective.

Coeliac disease is only a part of gluten-sensitivity

Yes, there is now a new understanding about the concept of being gluten-sensitive. It is much more than coeliac disease. Coeliac disease is only part of the picture. Let's look at this picture in more detail.

3. What are the symptoms?

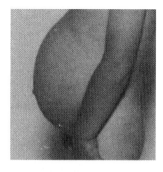

What symptoms would you get?

Until recently, coeliac disease was considered to be purely a gastro-intestinal problem. This is because, historically as we have seen, the predominant symptoms of established disease were a gut disturbance: diarrhoea and malnutrition. However, this viewpoint is rapidly changing. Being gluten-sensitive but *without* gut symptoms or gut damage is now a widely recognised problem.

What is the difference between gluten-sensitivity and coeliac disease?

It is only over the last decade that the blood tests have become universally available. Whole populations have now been screened for the gluten and tissue damage blood tests. This has led to a much better understanding about gluten-sensitivity and coeliac disease. The data for this is presented in Chapter 8.

Being gluten-sensitive has caused a change in thinking

Being gluten-sensitive is related to the harmful effects of gluten on the *whole* body. By contrast, coeliac disease is specifically about the gut damage and malabsorption. This concept has led to a major revision of diagnosis and management.

Coeliac disease

Coeliac disease is a *gastro-intestinal* disease. It is identified when there is damage to the small intestinal mucosa (skin) from the toxic effects of gluten in the diet. The diagnosis requires a small bowel biopsy by way of an endoscopy. The damaged appearance of the bowel is called "villus atrophy" (explained in Chapter 4). One of the problems is that such tissue damage can be difficult to pick up by just looking down a microscope. Early on in the progression of coeliac disease, inital small bowel biopsies might be normal.

The gut damage of coeliac disease can now be accurately measured by blood tests that detect tissue damage. These tissue damage blood tests are a positive EMA and tTG antibody tests (fully explained in Chapter 5). These "tissue damage" blood tests are strongly associated with the coeliac gut damage. This gut damage is completely reversible by going onto a strict gluten-free diet.

Coeliac disease is also strongly associated with the HLA types DQ2 and DQ8 (a genetic predisposition for coeliac disease).

Gluten-sensitivity

Simply, you are gluten-sensitive when your symptoms are provoked by gluten. This is usually associated with elevated levels of IgG-gliadin and/or IgA-gliadin antibodies. However, the upper small bowel biopsy can appear quite normal.

Symptoms disappear on a gluten-free diet

In some cases, being gluten-sensitive can be the prodrome of full-blown coeliac disease. Thus, if gluten is continued in the diet, then gluten-sensitivity will progress over time to cause gut damage. These people would then eventually be diagnosed as having coeliac disease.

However, most people who are gluten-sensitive *do not* develop any gut damage. This means that when a small bowel biopsy is performed, the absence of tissue damage *cannot* be used to exclude the gluten-sensitive condition. A normal small bowel biopsy can only exclude the presence of coeliac disease at the time of the biopsy.

Gluten-sensitivity is not so closely associated with the HLA type. However, more research is needed on this aspect.

What are the classic symptoms?

There is a large varied list of symptoms that are experienced by sufferers who are gluten-sensitive or who have coeliac disease. There is no way to distinguish these group by symptoms alone. The symptoms experienced by gluten-sensitive people and those with established coeliac disease are the same.

Some people will only have trivial symptoms, whilst others can have life-threatening illness. Have another look at the list of symptoms on the front page.

There are three categories of symptoms: general symptoms, specific gut symptoms, and finally the myriad of symptoms consequent from nutritional deficiencies. The symptoms that are experienced are as follows:

For babies and children

When babies start to eat cereals, their symptoms may include:

o   Become listless, miserable and irritable.
o   Go off their food and lose their appetite.
o   Grow poorly (poor weight gains, failure to thrive).
o   Have short stature (poor height gains).
o   Get diarrhoea (bulky, pale, smelly bowel motions).
o   Become constipated.
o   Have encopresis (soiling and loss of bowel control).
o   Show muscle-loss, particularly around the buttocks.
o   Have a 'pot-belly' due to abdominal distension.
o   Develop nutritional deficiencies (low iron, anaemia).
o   Have immunodeficiency (more illness and infections).
o   Poor muscle growth (weakness and developmental delay, muscle wasting).
o   Poor bone growth (osteoporosis).

Symptoms can develop at any age

Adults

Often, in adults, the predominant feature may not be the gut. A feeling of extreme tiredness is often the central feature. Intestinal symptoms may be completely absent. In other people, symptoms caused by malabsorption (the poor absorption of food) are their main complaints. The classic symptoms in adults include:

o   Tiredness and fatigue.
o   Diarrhoea or constipation.
o   Anaemia.
o   Mouth ulcers and sore tongue.
o   Heartburn, abdominal pains, bloating.
o   Weight loss.
o   Infertility.
o   Bone pain from osteoporosis.
o   Arthritis.
o   Weak muscles (myopathy).
o   Damaged nerve function (neuropathy).
o   Dermatitis herpetiformis (an itchy vesicular rash).

Symptoms range from trivial to very serious

The harm that gluten can inflict is widespread. Gluten can attack many regions of your body. This includes your brain, your skin and your joints. I call these the gluten-sensitive target organs, which are explained on the next page. Also, the severity of symptoms varies. Some people have mild symptoms while others can be severely ill at diagnosis.

You cannot distinguish the differences between coeliac disease and gluten-sensitivity from the symptoms alone. It is crucial to get the blood tests in order to sort out the diagnosis.

The ten target organs

The diagram puts the gluten symptoms in context. I have grouped these symptoms into ten "target" organs in your body that can be harmed by gluten. Each target organ is identified by a diamond box. As you can see, the small bowel is only one of these target organs. In this scheme, coeliac disease is just a small part of the gluten-sensitive spectrum. These ten target organs are:

Gut related symptoms

1. Mouth — ulcers, runny nose, sore throat.
2. Oesophagus — gastro-oesophageal reflux, heart burn, swallowing difficulties.
3. Stomach — indigestion, slow emptying, gastritis.
4. Small bowel — coeliac disease (enteropathy), malabsorption, diarrhoea.
5. Colon — diarrhoea and constipation, bloating, low immune function.
6. Rectum — constipation, soiling (encopresis).

Other symptoms

7. Brain — disturbed behaviour, migraine, grumpy, tired, headache, depression, mood disorders, ataxia, autism, epilepsy, Attention Deficit Hyperactivity Disorder (ADHD).
8. Skin — Dermatitis Herpetiformis, eczema.
9. Immune — run-down, low immunity, recurrent infections.
10. Growth — poor height and weight (short and/or thin).

Nutritional consequences

In addition to damage to these target organs, there are the nutritional consequences of a poorly functioning gut. These problems include:

Bones and joints — osteoporosis, bone and joint pain.
Nutritional deficiency — anaemia, osteoporosis, low levels of vitamins and minerals.
Infertility

Ten gluten-sensitive target organs

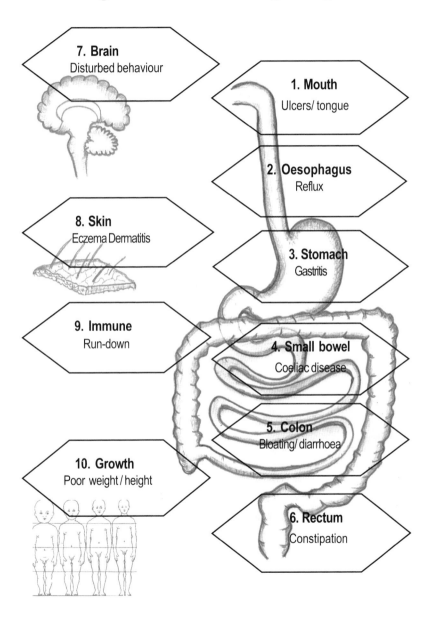

7. Brain
Disturbed behaviour

1. Mouth
Ulcers/ tongue

2. Oesophagus
Reflux

8. Skin
Eczema Dermatitis

3. Stomach
Gastritis

9. Immune
Run-down

4. Small bowel
Coeliac disease

5. Colon
Bloating/ diarrhoea

10. Growth
Poor weight / height

6. Rectum
Constipation

Can gluten-sensitivity affect your brain?

Yes! Gluten-sensitivity can definitely affect the brain. It causes small children irritability and they get really cranky. As they get older this can present as hyperactivity because gluten can upset their brain function. They are hyperactive because their brain is not happy. These children cannot concentrate well. They have a short fuse, they have tantrums, and they fight with their siblings and parents.

Gluten can affect the brain

This gluten affect on the brain can later give way to headaches and migraines. Gluten often makes you feel lethargic, moody and depressed. This is in addition to your physical weakness from any nutritional deficiency.

Symptoms of anxiety, mood swings and depression are also features of being gluten-sensitive. Neurological dysfunction can precede coeliac disease. However, it can also be the only manifestation of being gluten-sensitive.

A high prevalence of circulating antigliadin antibodies (IgG-gliadin and/or IgA-gliadin) has been found in patients with neurological dysfunction of "obscure aetiology". In one study 57% had positive antigliadin antibodies compared with only 12% in normal controls (normal controls had no neurological symptoms). But here is the interesting information regarding gluten-sensitivity: of the antibody positive patients, only 35% of these neurological patients had histological evidence of coeliac disease by biopsy. The remaining 65% had what they called "gluten-sensitivity". In this group, the target organ was their brain. Likewise, in dermatitis herpetiformis, the target organ is the skin (often with no gut damage).

The exciting news is that a large proportion of these patients recovered when they went onto a strict gluten-free diet.

Gluten can cause migraine

These findings yet again question the limited view of some that gluten-sensitivity can be confirmed only if coeliac disease (predominantly a gut condition) is demonstrated by biopsy. IgG-gliadin antibodies appear to have a high sensitivity not only for patients with coeliac disease but also for those with minimal or no bowel damage. The principal target organ can be the cerebellum (in the brain) or peripheral nervous system.

Brain symptoms disappear on a gluten-free diet

In support of this thinking, many of these neurological patients had an HLA genotype in keeping with coeliac disease. Many people who have migraines are also gluten-sensitive and fully recover on a gluten-free diet.

I believe that gluten-sensitivity could be thought of as a brain disease in some people. My hypothesis is that the symptoms from gluten occur through its action on the nervous system". In other words, gluten-sensitivity is a brain condition.

I propose that gluten can injure the nervous networks that control the gut's functions. This malfunction subsequently leads to all of the gut symptoms that have been described. In addition, gluten also directly affects the brain, which leads to the primary neurological symptoms that are so commonly seen with gluten-sensitivity. I have written this up, with the supporting medical literature, in the book: "Full Of It! The shocking truth about gluten".

What is dermatitis herpetiformis?

Dermatitis herpetiformis is one of the many problems caused by gluten-sensitivity.

Dermatitis herpetiformis is a very itchy skin condition. It can start suddenly. It tends to affect the elbows, knees, buttocks, scalp, and back. It begins as little bumps that then change into little blisters.

Gluten can cause itchy skin

The condition is thought to be caused by tiny clumps or deposits under the skin. These deposits are made up by a combination of IgA-gliadin and gluten (these deposits are also called immune-complexes). These deposits occur as a result of eating gluten. These deposits take a very long time to clear up once you start on a gluten-free diet. It may take up to ten years before you make a full recovery.

Interestingly, most people with dermatitis herpetiformis do not have troublesome gut symptoms. However, most do have some damage in their intestine. About 5% of coeliac patients develop dermatitis herpetiformis. Sometimes it can even develop *after* starting the gluten-free diet. This is probably due to the long lasting nature of the IgA immune-complex deposits.

Eczema

The skin is often a target organ in gluten-sensitivity. So, eczema can also be precipitated by gluten. Therefore, people with persistent eczema should get a blood test for their IgG-gliadin levels. This is a common manifestation of gluten-sensitivity.

4. Do I need a biopsy?

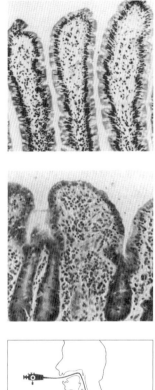

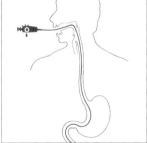

How do you make a diagnosis?

It is very important to make an accurate diagnosis for both coeliac disease and gluten-sensitivity.

However, the important message of this book is that it is very common to be gluten-sensitive *without* having any bowel abnormalities. This is a relatively new concept.

If someone is incorrectly put onto a gluten-free diet, without adequate evidence, then this can have a big social impact on that person, without the ensuing benefits. Moreover, once going on a gluten-free diet this is usually for a lifetime. Thus, going "gluten-free" should not be taken lightly.

Accurate diagnosis is important

In the past, the test for coeliac disease was centred on the small bowel biopsy. In addition, there were other investigations that looked for evidence of malabsorption (e.g. fat in the stool, blood tests for vitamin levels, and the xylose absorption test). These gut tests were developed prior to the availability of any blood tests.

To warrant such investigations (which could be expensive and time consuming), the patients had to have sufficient symptoms indicative of significant gut disease and malabsorption. A major problem for these tests were that they were not specific for coeliac disease. These tests were not done on children or adults until they were quite unwell with intestinal manifestations.

The non-specific nature of these tests led to what is called the three-biopsy protocol.

What is the three-biopsy protocol?

In 1969, in Interlaken, a beautiful town in Switzerland, a group of prominent gastroenterologists in paediatrics got together to work out a scheme to reliably diagnose coeliac disease. This was well before any blood tests came into the picture and before it was understood that gluten could commonly cause disorders outside the gut.

The object of the exercise was to unambiguously diagnose coeliac disease – also called gluten-sensitive enteropathy (enteropathy means the damage to the small bowel mucosa).

To diagnose coeliac disease with certainty, it was considered necessary to perform a total of *three* small bowel biopsies – on and off gluten.

The rationale for the three-biopsy protocol is as follows.

Biopsy-One:

First, you needed to suspect that a child might have coeliac disease. The child would usually present with lots of pale sloppy "poos", with a big tummy and not growing well. Gut symptoms were the focus. Also this child might be irritable and cranky. Often there would be coexisting nutritional deficiency. They would undergo their first small bowel biopsy to see whether the small bowel tissue was normal or abnormal.

If this biopsy was normal, then this child categorically *did not* have coeliac disease.

If the biopsy tissue was abnormal, then the child *might* have coeliac disease. This is because there are possible causes of abnormal small bowel tissue other than gluten toxicity.

41

Biopsy-Two:

If the first biopsy was abnormal, then this child was put onto a gluten-free diet. After a period of between six months and two years this child then had the second biopsy. This was to see if the gut had completely recovered on the gluten-free diet.

If the child had not got better (i.e. the second biopsy was still abnormal), then the child was considered not to have coeliac disease. Therefore, gluten was allowed back into the diet.

Biopsy-Three:

If the child had got better (that means that biopsy-two was normal), unfortunately, the diagnosis of coeliac disease could not yet be made. Even more evidence was required.

Therefore, this child was then put back onto gluten-containing foods again. The child would then be fed with gluten for three to six months (or less if the child got symptoms). Finally, they would have their third small bowel biopsy.

If biopsy-three was abnormal, then at last this child could be given the definite diagnosis of coeliac disease. However, since then it has been demonstrated that in some people it can take a decade for the small bowel damage to recur with a gluten challenge.

In summary, if this child had gone through that series of three biopsies, with the results: abnormal-normal-abnormal, then this child could be given the diagnosis of coeliac disease. This is because the first abnormal biopsy could be due to other conditions: it does not always come from gluten toxicity. However, in some children it was shown that it can take more than two years or more before definitive changes could develop in the small bowel tissue again.

What does a small bowel biopsy show?

Let us now look at the small bowel biopsy in more detail.

Look at your hand, what can you see? Skin! Dry skin with finger-prints. Now, look in the mirror and open your mouth – now you can see wet skin. The skin in your mouth is wet. That wet skin goes all the way down your intestinal tubes until it reaches your bottom end. Wet skin is called mucosa. It lines all of the tubes in your body. The individual cells in the mucosa are called epithelial cells.

When you take a microscope and look down on the wet skin (mucosa) of the small bowel (where the small bowel biopsy samples come from), it looks like this picture. It has undulating hills (the villi) and valleys (the crypts).

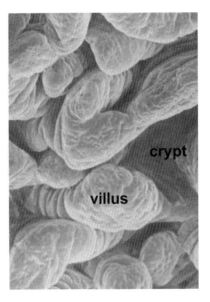

This is looking at the normal small bowel mucosa through a microscope: looking down on the villi and into the crypts.

Next, if you cut across the mucosa and look side-on, you will be able to see the normal villus (villi is the plural) which are finger-like projections. The picture below is an example of *normal small bowel tissue.*

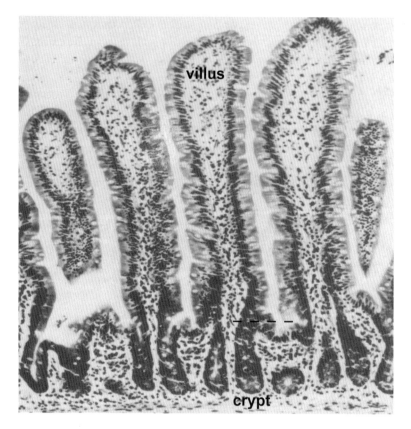

This is an example of a *normal* small bowel biopsy.
It shows the long finger-like villi and the crypt structure.
The villi are lined by individual epithelial cells.

The dashed line shows the junction between villus and crypt.

What are villi?

All the food that you eat has to be digested and absorbed somehow. Your villi do some of the digestion and most of the absorption. The nutrients, once they pass through the villi, get into the blood vessels and then get processed in your liver.

Villi absorb the food nutrients

The valleys at the bottom of the villi are called the crypts. The new epithelial cells are continually produced in these crypts.

These new cells slowly travel up the sides of the beautiful long villi, like a mini escalator ride. It takes two to three weeks for these cells to slowly migrate up to the top of the villus, doing their absorption job. Then, at the end of three weeks, they die and are shed off. They exhaust themselves. So, these villi have to be continuously replaced by new cells. The new cells are manufactured in the crypts, deep in the tissue.

In coeliac disease, the epithelial cells that line your villi get poisoned by the toxic effects of gluten. These poisoned cells die quickly. Because they die off quickly, the villi cannot grow very long – therefore, they do not absorb the food as well.

Also, the delicate supporting structure that supports the villi (the endomesial muscle) is damaged. This makes villi growth impossible.

Because of all of this damage from gluten, the crypts now have to work overtime to produce even more cells to line your villi. Thus the crypts keep on enlarging and getting deeper.

What does an abnormal biopsy look like?

Because the poisoned epithelial cells cannot produce proper villi, you get stumpy, sick looking villi. This is called *subtotal villus atrophy.* The epithelial cells are very damaged.

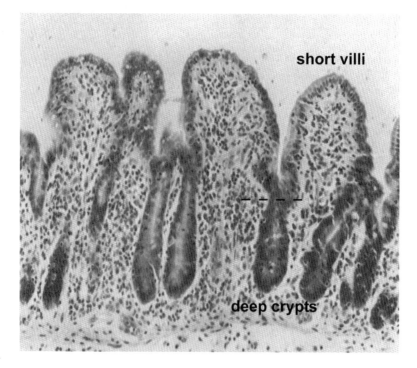

This is an example of an abnormal small bowel biopsy.
This shows *subtotal villus atrophy.*
Shortened villi and deepened crypts.

The dashed line shows the junction between villus and crypt.

What is a flat biopsy?

If the gluten toxicity continues (by staying on a normal diet), the villi become even more severely damaged. The most severe damage is called *total villus atrophy*. With such severely damaged gut tissue, the villi are unable to absorb your food nutrients. You are certain to experience nutritional deficiencies.

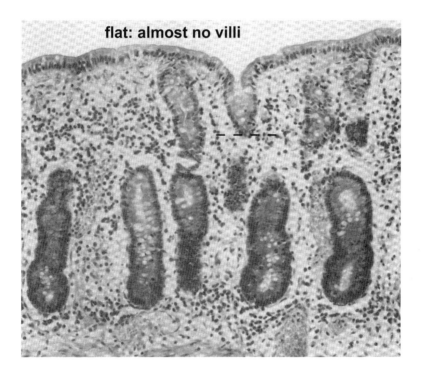

flat: almost no villi

This is an example of a very abnormal small bowel biopsy.
This shows *total villus atrophy*.
The villi have almost disappeared and the crypts are very deep.

The dashed line shows the junction between villus and crypt.

What do the disaccharidase tests measure?

Information about the *function* of the small bowel can also be obtained by small bowel biopsy.

The disaccharidase tests measure the enzymes that digest sugars in the small intestine. This is the activity of the lactase, sucrase, and maltase enzymes. This test needs a living piece of bowel mucosa to accurately measure the activity of these enzymes.

Disaccharidases digest sugars

These sugar enzymes are produced at the tip of the villi. When there is only subtle disturbance to the bowel, the damage might not show up as abnormal histology. But the damage may be enough to cause reduction in lactase and other enzyme activity.

The specific enzymes and their related sugars are:
o   The enzyme *Lactase* digests the sugar *Lactose*.
o   The enzyme *Sucrase* digests the sugar *Sucrose*.
o   The enzyme *Isomaltase* digests the sugar *Maltose*.

Sugar enzyme function is always affected when there is significant histological damage.

Low levels of these enzymes is the cause of some of the diarrhoea and bloating. The poor sugar absorption is the reason why milk (which contains lactose) is often not tolerated. Usually, on a gluten-free diet, these sugars can again be eaten without any problems.

Small bowel biopsy is very important

Should everyone have a small bowel biopsy?

No. In my opinion, not everyone needs to have a small bowel biopsy. However, it is an extremely important investigation. It should not be rejected lightly.

Currently, the guidelines that I use to decide on who should have a biopsy are as follows. I advise a small bowel biopsy for the following groups:

o   All children and adults who have elevated tTG or EMA antibodies.

o   In children who have substantially elevated IgA-gliadin levels (usually IgG-gliadin is also up).

o   In children with no family history with symptoms and substantially elevated IgG-antigliadin levels.

o   In children who are failing to thrive (poor growth) and who have negative gluten and tissue antibody markers.

In my experience, the biopsy is usually histologically normal in children, over two years of age, who have minor symptoms but have only moderately elevated IgG-gliadin.

However, endoscopy is not only about the small bowel. It also gives the opportunity to look for inflammation in the oesophagus and stomach. Many of these gluten-sensitive children present with symptoms of gastro-oesophageal reflux or gastritis.

To summarise, performing a small bowel biopsy is mostly about getting a sample of tissue from the upper small bowel to see what state the gut mucosa is in. An abnormal small bowel (coeliac disease) means a life-time gluten-fre diet.

However, a lot more information about the health of the upper gut can be derived from an endoscopy. It is a vital test. It is important that each person is assessed as an individual and that the decision about their biopsy criteria is fully discussed.

How accurate is the biopsy result?

Unfortunately, the biopsy is not a completely accurate test. It cannot be regarded as the absolute gold standard. In non-speciality pathology departments, studies suggest that up to 20% of the reports are falsely negative. That means that the minor abnormalities in the tissue have been overlooked and thus reported as normal.

Endoscopy is an important investigation

It is also very important to take the biopsy tissue from the correct location: that is in the duodenal bulb. Tissue taken lower down (from the distal duodenum or proximal jejunum) may be normal. Tissue damage might not extend very far down early in the disease process.

Finally, in early coeliac disease, the damage may be functional only: that means that the tissue histology early on will be normal. Some times the term "latent coeliac " is used.

Have the blood tests changed this approach?

Yes! Coeliac blood test markers have dramatically changed the rationale for doing a biopsy. The blood tests have been developed since the 1980s.

Slowly, there has been an erosion of the three-biopsy approach. Initially, the biopsy was stated to be the "gold standard" to diagnose (or refute) coeliac disease. So, logically, the new blood tests were compared to the biopsy results. The blood tests were analysed with regard to how accurately they were able to predict an abnormal biopsy.

However, by the 1990s, blood tests were being very widely used, and the justification of doing all three biopsies was being seriously questioned. The dogma of the three-biopsy protocol was steadily undermined and now is obsolete.

The tTG (tissue Transglutaminase) antibody has been identified as the most sensitive antibody marker for tissue damage in coeliac disease. In other words, tTG is a very accurate marker for gut damage in gluten-sensitivity. Some now claim that a high tTG level is evidence enough for coelaic disease.

All previous thinking had been orientated around the belief that coeliac disease is a condition diagnosed by an *abnormal small bowel biopsy*. It is not surprising that everyone has focused on the gut.

This focus on gut disease has come from the 120 years of this gut disease description, and also the 60 years of understanding about the gut effects of gluten. Finally there has been 40 years of examining abnormal small bowel biopsies.

However, there is now the new information to consider. It is now clear that being gluten-sensitive is much more than having a gut disease.

Gluten-sensitivity is more than a gut disease

Gluten-sensitivity can have extensive effects throughout the body. The advent of the blood tests has shown that there is a lot more going on. So, now a big question in "coeliac disease" is: "What is the meaning of the anti-gliadin antibodies, especially when the tTG results are negative?"

Let us look at the interpretation of the blood tests in much more detail.

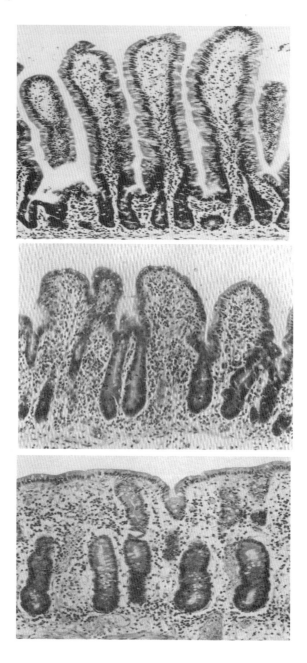

5. What do blood tests measure?

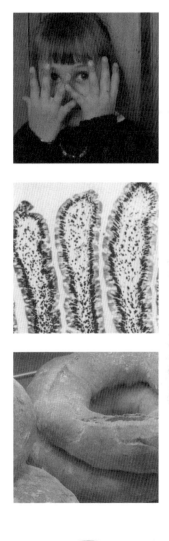

How useful are the blood tests?

The coeliac and gluten blood test markers have been progressively developed over the last twenty years. This has radically changed the understanding of gluten-sensitivity.

There are two different groups of antibodies

These blood tests can be divided into two groups. They measure quite different phenomena:

o   Gluten (food) antibodies.
o   Tissue (gut damage) antibodies.

What do the *gluten* antibodies mean?

The anti-gliadin antibodies (sometimes abbreviated as AGA, or more simply known as "gliadin" antibodies) are antibodies which are directed against gluten or gliadin *in the diet.* Gliadin is a specific protein that is part of gluten. There are two types of these antibodies: IgG-gliadin and IgA-gliadin. These antibodies are made by your immune system against the gluten that comes from wheat, rye and barley.

Gluten antibodies are diet related

These antibodies are called either *anti-gliadin antibodies* (there are two types – *IgG-gliadin* and *IgA-Gliadin* antibodies). These tests are very sensitive. But they are poor predictors of people who have coeliac disease (those who have the histological small bowel damage).

However, these tests are nearly always strongly positive in people with coeliac disease who are not on a gluten-free diet. On a strict diet, these antibody levels will begin to fall within a few months.

IgA-gliadin antibody: The IgA-gliadin antibody is a useful marker of gluten reactions. However, it does not become positive in everyone who has coeliac disease. If it is elevated, then you are very likely to have symptomatic gluten-sensitivity. This test can be used for monitoring compliance when on a gluten-free diet.

IgG-gliadin antibody: If the IgG-gliadin antibody is high, then this indicates the development of a gluten-sensitivity. With on-going eating of gluten, established full-blown coeliac disease could develop over many decades in those who are genetically susceptible. But in my experience, the great majority of people who have only raised IgG-gliadin antibody tests are gluten-sensitive but do not have coeliac disease.

I have organised small bowel biopsy investigations on many hundreds of children who have had bowel symptoms in association with elevated IgG-gliadin antibodies, but who had normal levels of tissue antibody markers (see below). In my experience, nearly all of these children have had normal small bowel tissue. However, most also symptomatically respond to a gluten-free diet. That is, they get better when off gluten.

IgG-Gliadin antibody is a very useful test

So the question at this point in time (for children who have symptoms, with a negative biopsy and a positive IgG-gliadin antibody test) is – do these children have coeliac disease? The answer will depend upon who you ask. I call these children *gluten-sensitive*. Some of these children will be *potential* or *latent* coeliacs. Remember that coeliac disease is a disease in progress. It takes time to develop. The HLA test can give additional information on the likelihood of developing coeliac disease.

What do *tissue* antibodies mean?

The Endomysial antibody (abbreviated as EMA) and tissue-transglutaminase antibody (abbreviated as tTG) are directed against the damaged endomysial muscle *in the tissue* of the bowel. These antibodies are made by your immune system to attack the gut-muscle tissue protein.

Tissue antibodies are a response to mucosal damage

In coeliac disease, there is an overreaction of the immune system. A harmful immune reaction occurs at the intestinal lining – the mucosa. This involves inflammatory cells and the production of antibodies. This abnormal immune response is triggered by the presence of gliadin (the name given to a component of gluten).

The tissue damage is caused by the immune system. It erroneously attacks parts of the delicate supporting structures surrounding the muscle fibres in the gut tissue. This structure is called the endomysium. The inflammation in the endomysial tissue results in the production of the anti-endomysial antibodies. This is what the blood test identifies and is the reason why people with coeliac disease (who have damaged small bowel tissue) have antibodies to a muscle tissue (endomysium).

EMA (Endomesial antibody): The endomysium is the delicate tissue that surrounds and supports the muscle fibres. The endomesial antibody (EMA) is an IgA-based antibody. It is an auto-antibody. That means it is an abnormal antibody directed against your own tissues. Until recently, the EMA had been found to be the most specific blood test for screening populations for coeliac disease (damaged bowel). For example, if you want to look at all the people in your town and find out who has coeliac disease, the most cost effective way of doing it was by just measuring everybody's EMA levels. This test generally becomes negative following 12–18 months on a gluten-free diet.

However, there are a number of problems with the EMA test. It is an immuno-histo-chemical assay. It uses either monkey oesophagus or human umbilical cord. The blood sample and chemicals are put onto this tissue and observed under a microscope. Thus the test is prone to technical error, inconsistent results and it is time-consuming.

In addition, in children under two years old this test cannot be relied upon to give an accurate indication of tissue damage.

ttG (tissue Transglutaminase) antibody: There is a special enzyme that is present in muscle tissue – this enzyme is called tissue transglutaminase. It appears that this enzyme can readily combine with gliadin. Somehow, this combination makes ttG more easily recognised by the body's immune system. This was discovered in 1997.

---

ttG antibody accurately indicates tissue damage

---

ttG has been shown to be the antigen that is recognised by endomesial antibodies in people with coeliac disease. Currently, a high level of ttG (tissue transglutaminase) antibody (which is also an IgA based antibody) in the blood is the most accurate blood test to make the diagnosis of coeliac disease in an individual.

If you have got a positive ttG antibody test, then there is about a 95% chance (but still not a 100%) that you will have an abnormal biopsy, with the telltale signs of coeliac disease. IgA antibodies to tTG become negative 9–24 months after commencement of a gluten-free diet.

The measurement of tTG is not without problems. Antigens used in the various test kits vary in their source and also arbitrary units are used to denote the positive value. So these factors contribute to the variations in sensitivity, specificity and predictive values that are reported. tTG can also be positive in other chronic inflammatory conditions. High levels have been reported in association with chronic liver disease and inflammatory bowel disease.

Also, tTG cannot be relied upon to always be present in early coeliac disease in young children under two years.

Finally, all tests that measure IgA based antibodies are of no value in a person who is deficient at producing IgA which is found in about 10% of coeliacs. Therefore, it is important to measure the total IgA levels as well as the specific antibodies.

How reliable are these "coeliac" blood tests?

To answer this question, you first have to examine another question: "With what are you to compare the blood tests?" The standard way of looking at their value has been to make a comparison with small bowel biopsy damage.

Using such comparisons, the table gives an indication of the reliability of the IgG-gliadin, IgA-gliadin and endomesial antibodies (EMA) and tissue transglutaminase (tTG).

First, each of these antibody tests provides a range of *specificity* for coeliac disease. This means that if you have coeliac disease, then this is your liklihood of having a positive blood test. The tTG and EMA antibodies have the highest specificity of up to 98–100%. In other words, only 0–10% of coeliacs have a negative tTG or EMA test (and this may to some extent be due to a general IgA deficiency).

	% of Specificity	% of Sensitivity
IgG-gliadin	60–92%	85–90%
IgA-gliadin	80–94%	80–95%
EMA	90–98%	80–98%
tTG	95–100%	80–100%

The other measurement of accuracy is the *sensitivity* which varies again depending on the study group and the test system that is used. Sensitivity is interpreted as follows: if you have a positive blood test, the chances that you have coeliac disease is given by the sensitivity figure. The tTG and EMA are again the most sensitive tests.

There are two reasons for the lower accuracy of the anti-gliadin antibodies. First, they can develop early in the disease. If a biopsy is performed *before* tissue damage becomes evident, then there will not yet be a diagnosis of coeliac disease. Therefore, the blood test is considered to be poor in sensitivity.

Second, this table relates to coeliac disease and not to gluten-sensitivity. The sensitivity levels would be much higher if the comparisons had been made with people who had symptomatic improvement on a gluten-free diet, whether or not the biopsy was abnormal.

When compared to adults, the tTG and EMA tests are less specific and less sensitive in children younger than two years old. It turns out that about 5% of people with coeliac disease will not have high tTG or EMA levels at diagnosis. =The younger children have more negative tests than the adults.

Have blood tests replaced the need for biopsy?

These coeliac blood test markers may ultimately be considered reliable enough for the majority of people never to need a duodenal biopsy. But not yet. However, while the blood test is not foolproof, a high positive tTG is almost as good as a biopsy. A positive result is rarely wrong if there are high levels with association with high IgG-gliadin and gut symptoms.

However, when the tTG test is negative, coeliac disease cannot be ruled out. Therefore, it is always important to do an intestinal biopsy if there is any suspicion of coeliac disease. Blood tests are not one hundred percent reliable, especially in children.

HLA typing

HLA is the abbreviation for the "Histocompatibility Leucocyte Antigen". It is used primarily as a test in tissue typing. It is like an expanded blood-type test. In blood-typing, the main groups are ABO and Rh (positive or negative). The HLA typing system is for tissue typing. It is detailed and complex. Of interest, many HLA types have been associated with specific diseases.

It has been discovered that most patients with biopsy proven coeliac disease have the HLA class II haplotype: HLA-B8, DR3 (also known as DQ2 and DQ8).

Indeed, coeliac disease is very rare in people without the HLA-DQ2 (in full: DQA1*0501, DQB1*02) or DQ8 (in full: DQA1*03, DQB1*0302) heterodimers. The "wrong" genes are only found in about 3% of coeliacs.

This is the genetic basis which can explain the increased risk in first-degree relatives. About 10% of first degree relatives are also affected. In HLA-identical siblings, this risk rises to 30%. In identical twins, the risk goes up to 70%.

Damage to the small bowel is thought to be somehow related to the HLA system. When gluten gets into the mucosa of the small bowel, it is bound to these HLA molecules (they are positioned on macrophages, the white blood cells in your gut). In this way, gluten can get exposed to the immune mechanism (by way of the mucosal T cells). This process stimulates an inflammatory immune response. The outcome of all of this is the raised antibody markers and the subsequent typical villus atrophy.

It seems that the HLA type is not closely associated with the way that coeliac disease presents in an individual.

It may be that the people who have gluten-sensitivity, but who do not go on to get small bowel damage, do not have the matching HLA types to create this erroneous immune response. This is yet to be confirmed.

In the general population, about 20% carry this same HLA set. Therefore, other mechanisms must be involved with the development of coeliac disease. Only a few of the HLA DQ2 or DQ8 people get coeliac disease. There are likely to be additional but yet unidentified genes involved. The development of coeliac disease is also associated with the age of gluten exposure or perhaps with the protection of gluten toxicity by breastmilk.

HLA typing has a very useful contribution to make. It is used as another marker of coeliac status. However, on its own it cannot be used as a diagnostic test. It is a measure of genetic predisposition.

What if my blood tests are negative?

From this discussion, it is clear that the blood tests are extremely useful. However, there are a number of children who have all of the clinical symptoms and signs of coeliac disease but they have negative blood tests. These children need to have a small bowel biopsy. The blood tests cannot be totally relied upon.

As discussed in Chapter 4, even the small bowel biopsy is not a reliable test. Some children respond to a gluten-free diet although all of their endoscopy tests have been normal. The diagnosis and management of both coeliac disease and gluten-sensitive people is not straight forward.

My doctor won't do my IgG-gliadin test - why?

This is becoming a frequent question. Because of the relative accuracy of the tTG antibody for detecting coeliac disease in adults, many doctors are now abandoning the IgG-gliadin test. They have their minds fixed on the relationship between gut damage and coeliac disease. They are not tuned into the wider concept of gluten-sensitivity. The reasons why your doctor might not do the gluten blood test are:

o   Your medical practitioner is only looking for coeliac disease.

o   The most accurate blood test for coeliac disease is the tTG (or EMA).

o   The condition, gluten sensitivity (shown by high IgG-gliadin) is not yet widely recognised.

o   Laboratories around the world are abandoning the IgG-gliadin test in favour of the tTG antibody.

o   Medical practitioners have been trained to disregard IgG-gliadin results – they are told that it is a "non-specific" result without any clinical meaning.

o   Your medical practitioner may have a budget to consider and would not spend money on a test that was disregarded.

A patient said, "I went to my doctor for a blood test on gluten-sensitivity (following your guidelines) but my doctor didn't do the specific tests that I asked for (I actually showed him your letter). He told me that the results came back saying that I do not have coeliac disease. How do I get my doctor to do the tests that will determine whether I'm gluten-sensitive? Or do I need to see another doctor for that?"

Therefore, I recommend that you discuss the possible blood tests with your medical practitioner and laboratory *before* getting the blood taken. In my opinion, it is essential to get the IgG-gliadin antibody test. Without this result it is difficult to be sure about the diagnosis of gluten-sensitivity. Full recommendations and reasons for each blood test can be found at our website: www.doctorgluten.com.

Get the correct interpretation

Make sure that you know the true meaning of your blood tests. These tests are often misinterpreted. If you would like some help, then follow these steps:

o   Go to the webpage www.doctorgluten.com
o   Then, at Blood Test Results enter your test results
o   You will be sent an interpretation of your blood tests results and suggestions of what action you could take.

IgG-Gliadin antibody is a test for gluten-sensitivity

I am already on a gluten-free diet. Can I still have a blood test?

It depends how long you have been on a gluten-free diet. The blood tests for gliadin antibodies take about at least six months or more to change once you go gluten-free. They slowly go down as your body's immune system stops being stimulated by gluten.

So if you have only been gluten-free for a few weeks or months, then it is okay to get your blood tests. You do not have to go back and eat more gluten.

What evidence do you have that shows the IgG-gliadin test is useful?

I have over 500 people on gluten-free diets. But only 50 of these people have coeliac disease. The remainder are gluten-sensitive, with no evidence of any gut damage. However, when the two groups are compared, they cannot be distinguished by their symptoms alone.

For every one person diagnosed with coeliac disease (with blood tests and endoscopy), I see another nine people who have the same symptoms, but who are gluten-sensitive. They have high IgG-gliadin antibodies and feel remarkably better when they go on a gluten-free diet. I am convinced that they are gluten-sensitive - and so are these grateful people. The more you look for gluten-sensitivity, the more you will find it.

Do not go gluten-free without a blood test

I would like to repeat the importance of the tTG or EMA result. If you have a high tTG or EMA antibody test, then this indicates that you might have significant small bowel damage. This means that you might have coeliac disease. You should probably have a confirmatory small bowel biopsy (by endoscopy) *prior* to going gluten-free. You will need to discuss this with your doctor.

Get blood tests for gluten-sensitivity & coeliacs

I recommend that you do not go gluten-free without first having a full set of blood tests.

6. Is gluten-sensitivity life long?

Does gluten-sensitivity change over time?

To understand gluten-sensitivity, you need to be aware of the timeline of gluten-sensitivity and how sometimes it might progress to coeliac disease. Coeliac disease is a disease in progress, but most people who are sensitive to gluten do not develop coeliac disease. The first diagram depicts the sequence of events in a child with coeliac disease.

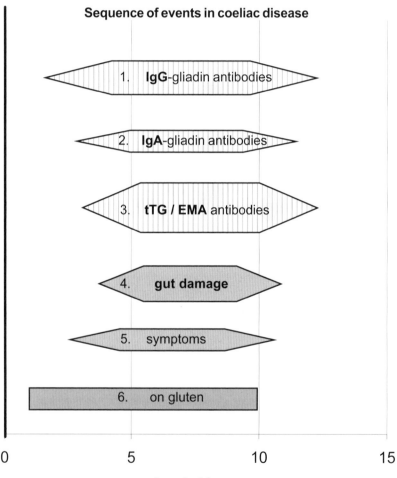

Sequence of events in coeliac disease

1. **IgG**-gliadin antibodies
2. **IgA**-gliadin antibodies
3. **ttG / EMA** antibodies
4. **gut damage**
5. symptoms
6. on gluten

0   5   10   15

Age in Years

A case study of coeliac disease

This story is about a girl who was eventually diagnosed as having coeliac disease when she was 10 years old. The top three light-shaded bars show the onset and progression of the antibody changes. The next two bars show when she developed gut damage and symptoms. The bottom bar indicates that she was first exposed to gluten at six months old, and consumed gluten products through until 10 years of age.

When do symptoms first appear?

In this scenario, she started to eat gluten foods from six months old (see bar 6 in the diagram). Her symptoms first became apparent at two years old (bar 5). These were initially intermittent abdominal pain, her bowel motions got a bit more sloppy, and she became more irritable.

Coeliac disease is a progressive condition

Her symptoms got slowly more severe as time went on. Temper tantrums and hyperactivity developed. Her growth also began to become more affected, especially her height. She looked a little thin. A pot tummy became a feature and she did not have much energy. Her malabsorption caused iron deficiency and low immune function.

At 10 years of age she had the appropriate blood tests showing the antibody markers for gliadin and tissue damage were raised (bars 1, 2 and 3). She had an endoscopy and her bowel showed subtotal villus atrophy (bar 4). Coeliac disease was diagnosed. Following this diagnosis, she immediately went on a gluten-free diet. Her symptoms receded, disappearing within a month. Her gut damage healed within three months. It took a few years for her antibodies to return to normal levels. We will now look at her story in more detail.

When do blood tests first become positive?

In the diagram, time zero is the birth of this girl who was susceptible to gluten. She had the HLA type DQ2. She was a brand new baby. No food had ever passed through her lips before.

She is put on the breast. It is assumed that breast milk is gluten-free. However, breast milk *does* contain small amounts of gluten in mothers who are consuming substantial amounts of gluten.

The answer to this question about the effects of gluten through breastmilk is presently unknown. I speculate that there can be enough gluten in some breast milk to upset some babies. This means that babies who are drinking breast milk are not on a gluten-free diet..

You cannot have coeliac disease at birth

When this baby is born, she has a hundred years of life ahead of her. She happens to have a genetic predisposition for coeliac disease. This is determined by her HLA type.

She is fed gluten from the age of six months through to 10 years of age. We know that she is eventually going to get coeliac disease. The tricky question is this: "When does she have enough evidence to be diagnosed as having coeliac disease?" Let us go through the development of her coeliac disease, step by step.

At birth

At birth, she had a beautiful, normal gut. The process of becoming gluten-sensitive probably begins as soon as gluten is introduced into her diet (perhaps even via breastmilk). Gluten, when it gets into her body through the mucosa of her gut, begins to react with her immune system and produce antibodies. This immune reaction takes quite a long time to get established. In some people it takes decades. In this girl it took over a year.

The first antibodies

The first antibody to develop (of those that we are aware of and that we can currently test for in the laboratory) is usually the IgG-gliadin antibody. This antibody can be detected in some babies at 6 months of age or even younger. However, in other cases it can take a lot longer to develop. It can take years to appear.

IgG-gliadin antibody usually appears first

In this girl, the IgG-gliadin first appears elevated at two years old (depicted by bar 1 in the diagram). The age of developing this immunological sensitivity to gluten will depend upon many factors including: the age of the introduction of gluten into the diet; the amount of gluten consumed; the degree of susceptibility of the child; length of breastfeeding; and the responsiveness of the child's immune system. Sometimes, other gut conditions such as food allergy and gastroenteritis may contribute.

More antibodies

Antibody development is usually sequential. After IgG-gliadin antibodies have developed, the next antibody to develop is often IgA-gliadin. This girl had a positive IgA-gliadin at four years old (bar 2). In others, this may develop years later. Some people never develop the IgA-gliadin antibody.

As the years go by, these antibody levels slowly get higher as gluten is continued in the diet. The important thing to grasp is this: that at any point in time, as we take blood tests on this girl, year by year, the results of the panel of antibodies is going to look different. Population studies suggest that the IgG-gliadin is likely to be first elevated before school age.

Antibody development is usually sequential

Next, come the tissue antibodies: endomesial (EMA) and tissue transglutaminase (tTG) antibodies (bar 3 in the diagram). These antibodies measure the same thing: the degree of bowel damage. In this girl they developed by five years old. Usually at this stage there are troublesome symptoms, but not always. Some people, even with high antibody levels and gut damage, seem to have remarkably few symptoms. However, they nearly all feel a lot better when they go on to a gluten-free diet!

When does the biopsy first become positive?
It may take 1 year, 2 years, 10 years, 20 years, 30 years or even a lot longer before there is enough damage inflicted on the intestine (gut) by gluten, for it to show up as microscopic abnormalities. It is thought that with continued gluten intake, the gut damage becomes progressively worse. In this example, her bowel became abnormal at six years old (bar 4 in the diagram). At 10 years old she had her diagnostic biopsy.

The first changes are very subtle, with an increase in the inflammatory cells. Next, the villi become shortened and sick looking: so called *subtotal villus atrophy*. Eventually, the appearance of the bowel mucosa gets to its worst state: *total villus atrophy* (see the pictures in Chapter 4). If someone has an endoscopy, and the small bowel looks entirely normal, this *does not* rule out the possibility of coeliac disease in the future. It can take decades for the damage to develop and become established. So, it is important to continue to keep a high index of suspicion about the possibility of developing coeliac disease.

When do symptoms first develop?

This is a key question but perhaps the most difficult to answer. We first have to know what symptoms we are looking for. In this case study her symptoms began at two or three years old (bar 5 in the diagram). Until recently, coeliac disease was considered to be almost exclusively a gut (bowel) disease. However, from the above story, you can see that coeliac disease is a disease in progress. To complicate matters, the clinical entity of being gluten-sensitive has emerged. This will be explored in more detail later, below and in Chapter 8.

When did coeliac disease first start?

Can you answer this question: "When did this girl first get coeliac disease?" Currently, a gastroenterologist is only likely to make a definite diagnosis when there is evidence of microscopic bowel damage (that is: an abnormal small bowel biopsy). However, in my opinion, I would make a diagnosis of gluten-sensitivity as soon as there were symptoms that were associated with rising gluten antibodies. That is when she was two or three years old. This stage is often referred to as "potential" or "latent" coeliac disease.

Coeliac disease can appear at any age

This is because coeliac disease is a progressive condition. This child is likely to slowly develop more symptoms and progressively get worse and worse. Testing for her HLA type would give another clue. However, a biopsy done before four years of age in this girl would look normal.. The difficulty with diagnosis is that coeliac disease can present at any age. Although it is possible to get very unwell by nine months of age, other people might never show severe symptoms despite having bowel abnormalities.

People with coeliac disease are diagnosed at any age from 9 months through to 90 years of age. Some people are much more tolerant to gluten but, nevertheless, they still have the disease.

If we were to do a blood test on this child at three years of age, because she has had some symptoms over the last year, we would find that her IgG-gliadin was slightly raised. But her other antibody levels (IgA-gliadin and tTG) were within the normal range. At this point, we did not know her genetic make up and we did not know that in the future this girl was going to develop full-blown coeliac disease.

However, the evidence for coeliac disease becomes stronger and stronger as she gets progressively older. It is important to keep a close eye on such children if there are *any* suspicions of gluten intolerance.

Keep a close eye on possible gluten-sensitivity

A case study of gluten-sensitivity

Being gluten-sensitive is not the same as having coeliac disease. The body reacts in a different pattern. Although there is no gut damage, the symptoms can be very similar to that of coeliac disease. This is shown in the next diagram. I think that this different response is to some extent due to having a different genetic make up.

This case study is a boy who was eventually diagnosed as being gluten-sensitive at 10 years of age. He was started on gluten foods at 9 months old (see bar 6). By two years of age he was having mild symptoms (see bar 5). He had mild constipation and was increasingly irritable. He had a rather pale look and had developed a pot tummy. He was experiencing poor health, seeming to pick up everything that was going around. He was often on antibiotics for ear infections.

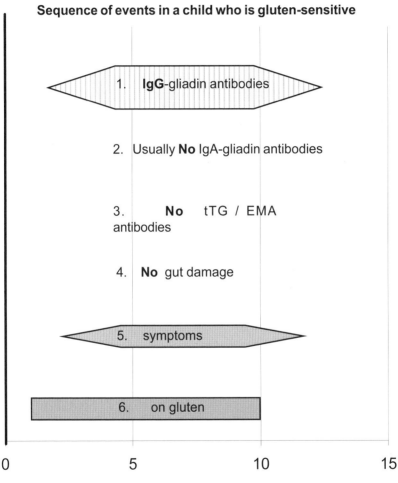

Sequence of events in a child who is gluten-sensitive

1. **IgG**-gliadin antibodies

2. Usually **No** IgA-gliadin antibodies

3. **No** tTG / EMA antibodies

4. **No** gut damage

5. symptoms

6. on gluten

0   5   10   15

Age in Years

By 8 years of age he was still frequently unwell and now beginning to slow down with his growth. He looked rather thin and appeared to be a little shorter than his school mates. By 10 years of age he began to complain of tummy aches. He was still having some constipation difficulties.

Eventually, I was asked to see him. He had a very high IgG-gliadin level (84 units) (see bar 1). His other antibody levels were within the normal range (IgA-gliadin 10 units and ttG 8 units) (bars 2 and 3).

Because of his long-standing symptoms and poor growth he went ahead for a small bowel biopsy. This was completely normal (see bar 4).

He then was started on a gluten-free diet for a three month trial. He experienced a dramatic response. Within a week he was feeling more energetic and soon began to eat more. His tummy pains disappeared and by another six weeks he no longer had any problems with his bowels. He became less irritable and his teacher asked his parents what had been happening at home.

Because of this impressive turnaround in his health, he began to doubt the value of the gluten-free diet. However, he learned his lesson quickly. At a birthday party he decided to have some normal sausages and birthday cake. Within two hours he had severe abdominal pains and vomited that night. He experienced a headache and became constipated for the few days. This is a typical response following gluten withdrawal. He was now even more sensitive to gluten.

He now remains gluten-free and he is pleased to be growing again. He is young enough to regain his lost height.

How common is coeliac disease?

Recent population studies in countries throughout the world are finding that about 1-in-100 people have evidence of coeliac disease (in this context this means intestinal damage from gluten). These studies have generally been based on doing population blood test screening.

Coeliac disease is very common

A two-stage antibody screening has been the usual strategy, often followed up by small bowel biopsy. Typically, the antibody testing is a combination of ttG (tissue transglutaminase) and EMA (endomesial antibody). However, this strategy of screening is not precise and it will significantly underestimate the size of the problem.

In a recent UK study, over 5,000 of 7-year-old children were tested. They found that 1% (that is 1-in-100) of these children had positive results. This study will underestimate the real prevalence of coeliac disease because it does not include those with positive IgG-gliadin levels who have yet to develop the tissue-damage markers.

These children with positive tests were generally smaller than those with normal tests. They also tended to have multiple symptoms of diarrhoea, vomiting, abdominal pain, and constipation. They did not have the classic appearance of coeliac disease. Only one of these children had attended their doctor for assessment of diarrhoea. The lesson from this study was that coeliac disease is extremely common. It is important to keep the possibility of this in mind when assessing anyone for persistent troublesome gut symptoms. A greater awareness is needed throughout the community.

How common is gluten-sensitivity?
People who are gluten-sensitive are seen even more commonly. The data behind the following estimate is given in Chapter 8. I have calculate that 1-in-10 people are gluten-sensitive. That is ten percent of the population. For every one coeliac that I see, I identify another nine who are gluten-sensitive.

Blood bank population studies show that 10% of "well" donors have elevated IgG-gliadin levels. Although these results have been disregarded as "non-specific", I think that these test results accurately describe the size of the problem.

I have found that 75% of the children that I see for a range of gastrointestinal and allergy problems have elevated IgG-gliadin antibody levels. A research group in the USA is also finding that children who are gluten-sensitive outnumber those with coeliac disease by ten-to-one. Some groups claim that it is even more common, affecting more than 20% of the population. The diagnosis and the management of people who are gluten-sensitive will tremendously improve the health of the population. The first step is to carefully document the problem and then to convince a sceptical medical community about it.

Is coeliac disease becoming more common?
Well, it depends how hard you look. The more you look the more you will find. A decade ago coeliac disease was thought to be an uncommon disease, with less that 1-in-1000 being affected. These studies were based on people being recognised by their gut symptoms and then having the diagnosis made by small bowel biopsy.

Hundreds of thousands remain undiagnosed

Now there are accurate blood tests available to pick up people with coeliac disease. These tests were not available 20 years ago. Recent studies find that coeliac disease affects 1-in-100 individuals, or even more. The "iceberg" is a common model used to describe the epidemiology of coeliac disease. This means that only a minority of individuals will have a clinically recognised disease. This explains the previous low prevalence figures prior to the blood test era. The remainder (those yet-to-be-diagnosed) greatly outnumber those who have been so far diagnosed. Coeliac disease is being discovered more frequently, and the community is becoming much more aware of this condition. But there is a very long way to go. So, nobody can definitely say if coeliac disease is actually more common. However, it is being recognised much more frequently. In addition, we are now talking about the entity of gluten-sensitivity.

One way to possibly reduce the problem of gluten-sensitivity is to delay the introduction of gluten into the diet. Perhaps by not giving gluten foods until 12 months of age. There is some evidence that gluten introduction is best started while you are still being breast fed. There is not yet enough information to give clear guidance on this aspect of dietary gluten. This widespread sensitivity to gluten may have been spurred on by the fast-food industry which is based on pizza bases and bread buns.

Does it run in families?

Yes, it does run in families. The incidence in first-degree relatives (parents, brother and sisters) is between 10–15% in a family member. So all immediate family members should be tested once someone else in their family is diagnosed.

All family members should be tested

How many people are still undiagnosed?
Unfortunately, there are huge numbers of people with undiagnosed gluten-sensitivity and coeliac disease. There are several reasons.

First, some people do not experience any symptoms. These people are usually found when they have been tested because they are a close relative of someone else with established coeliac disease. Another group are those who have been picked up by screening studies. Although these people do not have symptoms when tested, they might gradually develop symptoms as time goes by.

Second, many people do not get any noticeable symptoms on gluten, although most do have subtle symptoms when looked for. However, gluten is still damaging them. The classic example of this is short stature. This is a condition where children do not grow to their full potential – they are short. But they do not have any other recognised symptoms. All unexpectedly short people, despite their lack of symptoms, should be evaluated to see if they are gluten-sensitive.

Short people should have a gluten test

If they have blood tests, you may find that they have got high gluten markers. If they have endoscopy biopsy, they might have a very damaged gut. When they then go on a gluten-free diet, they often feel a lot better because they have always felt a bit down, but not known what it was like to feel well. If these people are not found until adulthood, they will not grow any more because their growing period has finished. Finding these gluten-sensitive children is urgent.

Third, the symptoms of those who are gluten-sensitive can be varied and subtle. Therefore, unless you have a very high index of suspicion of this condition, it will not be tested for. Therefore, it will be missed. The rule is – if gluten-sensitivity is a possibility, then do the blood test for it. This means IgG-gliadin, IgA-gliadin and tTG antibodies.

Can you go into remission?

This is a very hopeful question. It is often asked with the meaning "How long is it before I can start eating gluten again?" The answer, to some extent, depends upon the reasons and evidence for instigating the gluten-free diet.

However, the answer for nearly everyone is probably *never*. It is likely, that once sensitive to gluten, that this is a lifelong condition. In my experience, people who start a gluten-free diet usually choose to stay on a gluten-free diet.

If there has been small bowel tissue damage (as evidenced by an elevated tTG or small bowel biopsy), then it is highly recommended that you go gluten-free *lifelong*. Even small traces of gluten in the diet have been shown to continue the gut inflammatory processes. Just one gram of gluten per day is all that is needed to cause continued bowel damage.

Tiny amounts of gluten can cause damage

However, in the early phases of the process, when there is gluten-sensitivity (as evidenced by elevated IgG-gliadin and/or IgA-gliadin) but not established bowel damage, then going gluten-free might possibly interrupt the process. However, there is no information on this subject to make a firm opinion. My advice would be to accept being gluten-free as a way of life under these circumstances.

Do you grow out of it?

Following on from the above arguments, no, you do not grow out of it! If you did grow out of it, then the original diagnosis would be in doubt. You probably never had coeliac disease or were never gluten-sensitive.

There is another explanation for those people who seem to have grown out of it. These people may no longer experience symptoms from gluten, but they might still have the disease process going on silently inside them. They do not recognise that they are still being subtly affected. I do not believe that people grow out of being gluten-sensitive.

Gluten-sensitivity appears to be a lifelong condition

Remember that some people are quite tolerant to eating gluten, despite their blood and endoscopy tests being positive. Everybody is different, that is why it can be so elusive to diagnose.

Is my cancer risk increased with coeliac disease?

A big question is the one about the increased risk of cancer. People ask: "How much do I have to lower my gluten intake to lower my subsequent risk of bowel cancer?"

The classic malignancy associated with coeliac disease is a lymphoma of the small intestine (its full name is: enteropathy-associated T-cell lymphoma). However, cancers of the small intestine, oesophagus, and pharynx are also associated with coeliac disease.

The good news is that a strict gluten-free diet *does* protect against these malignancies. This has been shown in systematic longitudinal studies. The results indicate that if you are on a gluten-free diet for five years or more, then the risk of developing cancer is not increased when compared with the general population.

Five years gluten-free makes you normal

For children, put on a gluten-free diet, and staying on their gluten-free diet lifelong, the cancer issue is probably irrelevant. However, it is important for them to know about the cancer risk should they decide to abandon their diet.

This protective effect against cancer (and also against osteoporosis and other nutritional deficiencies) remains the strongest argument for total withdrawal of gluten from the diet of those sensitive to gluten.

Is wheat allergy different to gluten reactions?

Wheat allergy is a different type of reaction to gluten-sensitivity. Gluten is only one of many proteins that are contained in wheat. Every plant and animal food that you eat contains various proteins. Grains are quite rich in protein: about 10% of grain is protein.

One of the proteins in grain is gluten. But there are lots of other different proteins as well. Proteins are built up from long chains of molecules called amino-acids. If you are an allergic person, then you can potentially become allergic to almost any protein. And if you develop an allergy to wheat, it will probably be to one of the non-gluten proteins. That would mean that you could probably eat rye, barley and oats because these grains will not necessarily have the specific wheat protein that is making you allergic to wheat. However, there is a degree of cross-sensitivity.

Usually, a wheat allergy reaction causes more immediate reactions, and the symptoms are completely different to coeliac disease. A wheat allergy often starts with a rash or hives, followed by some facial swelling. Sometimes, wheezing and breathlessness are part of this reaction. Being gluten-sensitive is not regarded as an allergic reaction. However, it is an abnormal immune response.

With just positive blood tests can I go gluten-free?

I am a great believer in organising the small bowel biopsy in people who have a possibility of a gut abnormality. I think it is very important for their future. It gives some very useful information, at a specified time, on the status of their gut – whether or not they have any microscopic or functional damage. Currently, it is common practice to still confirm the diagnosis by endoscopy if there are elevations in the tTG or EMA antibodies.

It is a good idea to have a biopsy

However, once the biopsy is done, whether it is normal or abnormal, I advise that most people go onto a trial of a gluten-free diet for at least three months *if* they have elevated IgG-antigliadin markers *and* also have symptoms.

If you have been on a gluten-free diet for a couple of months before a biopsy has been contemplated, then it is pointless to do a biopsy looking for small gut damage – it will have already healed on the gluten-free diet.

There are not strict rules that suit everybody. Each person is unique. Each person needs to be assessed in relation to their own circumstances.

There is, understandably, some reluctance for people who are strongly suspected of having coeliac disease, to wait a long time to have an endoscopy while still on gluten. I encourage the parents to continue the gluten in their child's diet for another few weeks, so that they can have their endoscopy while on gluten. Under these circumstances, the parents feel that they are now poisoning their child.

Each person is unique

How often should you have blood tests done?
In Italy, there is a research group that has been carrying out screening tests for all school children at five years of age. They argue that this is the only way they can reliably detect coeliac disease in the community. But five years old is quite young to try and exclude coeliac disease.

Not all those who will develop coeliac disease will have detectable antibodies by five years of age. If you were to test those children again when they were ten, you would find some new children who were gluten-sensitive.

It is my view that you can never rule out the possibility of coeliac disease with absolute certainty unless you measure for the HLA associated markers. Even then a few people would be falsely reassured. What you can say, at the time of normal blood tests for coeliac markers, is that you are not gluten-sensitive at this time.

If there is continued suspicion, then doing coeliac marker blood tests every few years in children is worthwhile. In adults perhaps every five years.

A typical story

Coeliac disease is a disease in progress. I have seen several children with the following type of story.

I see these children at about 18 months of age. They have loose bowel motions and are not growing as well as expected. I organise some blood tests for coeliac antibodies and they are normal. However, because of concerns about their growth I organise a small bowel biopsy – and it is normal.

I see such children again at 4 years old because there are still minor concerns. We repeat the blood tests which now show slightly positive for IgG-gliadin. But the child shows no worsening of symptoms although the child is growing slowly. A decision is made to stay on gluten foods – and watch for a little longer.

Diagnosis can be a waiting game

Then, for the third time I see the child at 6 years old. There is not much clinical change: still some intermittent diarrhoea, still creeping along for growth. But now more irritable and cranky.

So the blood tests are done again. This time they show a much higher IgG-gliadin and a high tTG result. This is evidence of coeliac disease.

I organise a second small bowel biopsy and this time it is positive – there is a flat biopsy with subtotal villus atrophy. The child now has full-blown coeliac disease.

A gluten-free diet is started, the bowel motions become normal, the behaviour greatly improves. Over the next few years the height and weight begin to climb again.

By this time there are brothers and sisters about. Some have mild symptoms, others have no symptoms.

The next step is to do blood tests on the whole family. The result is that the family members have antibody evidence of varying degrees of gluten-sensitivity. So most of the family goes gluten-free – with everyone feeling a great deal better.

The ripple effect continues. Blood tests are now organised for the grandparents, aunts, uncles, nephews and nieces. Another group of people have been recognised to have gluten-sensitive symptoms. Some people are angry that it has taken so long for their condition to be recognised. Others are just thankful for feeling well for the first time in their lives.

Always be suspicious of gluten

That is the problem. Coeliac disease is a disease in progress. You need to be aware of it all the time. You cannot be reliably told that you will never have coeliac disease, especially if you have a family with coeliac disease or gluten-sensitivity. Moreover, about one in ten of the population is gluten-sensitive.

So how often should your child have blood tests? It mostly depends upon whether you or your child has any subtle symptoms. In my practice, I look at coeliac antibody markers every 6–12 months in a young child with symptoms but negative blood tests. I repeat the blood tests every 2–3 years in an older child with a suspicion of gluten-sensitivity but with previous negative blood tests. Lastly, I repeat blood tests every 1–2 years in a child without symptoms but with positive blood tests.

Do health professionals keep up with all this?

Information about every aspect of health and disease is expanding daily. You just cannot expect anyone to keep up with it all, it is just impossible. We remember much of what we are taught, and then, unless we are continually updating ourselves, we become stuck in history. Time stands still for that portion of our knowledge. Some things change faster than others.

Over the last few years, things have moved rapidly in the understanding of gluten-sensitivity. This knowledge is not held by everyone. This is a prime motive for writing this book. Information is on the move.

So it is not surprising that many health professionals still regard gluten-sensitivity as being "coeliac disease" – only a gut problem. Many medical people at the moment ridicule people going onto a gluten-free diet without histological evidence of coeliac disease. I am frequently criticised for my viewpoint. However, my clinical practice is based on 20 years of managing coeliac disease and the newly recognised group of gluten-sensitive people. My data is presented in detail in Chapter 8.

The world is shifting, everything is in motion. What we thought was right last year may be different this year. There is constantly new information, and the rules keep changing. So unfortunately, you cannot be secure that any advice that you are given is completely up-to-date. It is often a good idea to seek a second opinion.

Information is changing rapidly

7. What is gluten-free?

What does gluten-free mean?

Simply, on a gluten-free diet you will have to exclude *all* foods that contain gluten. This means excluding even tiny amounts of gluten. This is called "gluten-free" which is often abbreviated with the initals GF.

The common gluten-containing foods are ordinary wheat-based breads, cakes and any other product made from ordinary wheat-based flour.

Gluten-free removes all gluten from wheat, rye & barley

Nowadays, there are lots of excellent commercially available gluten-free products, such as flours, biscuits and pasta. In some countries, many of these GF foods are available on prescription for people who have coeliac disease.

How do I start on a gluten-free diet?

When you first hear that you (or your child) needs to go on to a gluten-free diet, it can be overwhelming. Often the first response that I hear is: "What a lot of foods that we have to cut out! What on earth can I eat?" However, there are excellent replacements for nearly everything. It is just a matter of slowly getting organised. It is often just a matter of swapping brands.

Take it slowly

It is not urgent to be totally free of gluten overnight. You can take your time. It does not have to happen immediately. Perhaps give yourself a month to make the transition to going completely gluten-free. It takes time to learn. The important thing to do is make a start.

The first thing to do is to focus on the obvious foods that are made from the gluten-grains: wheat, barley and rye. It is important to replace these grains with other cereals. Cereals are a valuable source of carbohydrates (for energy), fibre (for your bowels), and vitamins and minerals (for your nutritional health).

However, starting a gluten-free diet is also an opportunity to cut down on unnecessary refined carbohydrates that so easily creep into our diets.

We all make mistakes – it is part of learning

You will make mistakes. Everyone makes mistakes. This is inevitable. Nobody can be perfect. Give yourself lots of time to adjust.

How quickly should I feel better?
Usually, when you go gluten-free, you will feel magically better within one or two weeks. Then, it takes a few more weeks for the gut to get steadily better. Sometimes this might take up to three months. Although in adults, slow improvements can continue up to two years.

The exception seems to be with dermatitis herpetiformis. This can take several years (and maybe up to ten years) to resolve. It can even appear after you have started going gluten-free. The younger the person, the faster they get better. People who have had coeliac disease for decades sometimes do not get fully better. They have been damaged too much.

One of the major problems in children is their growth. If someone is on gluten, and they are not growing properly because of coeliac disease or gluten-sensitivity, if they go gluten-free they will start growing again. If you make those children unwell again by challenging with gluten (maybe for several months), this will stop them from growing. This is the very time that you want these children to grow!

In my opinion, it is very important *not* to challenge these children with gluten during their growing years.

You can eat nearly anything that is unprocessed

What can I eat?
A good place to start is with the food that you *can* eat! This is a short but complete list.

o   All unprocessed fruits.
o   All unprocessed vegetables and beans.
o   All unprocessed meats, fish, poultry, eggs.
o   All simple dairy products.
o   All unprocessed gluten-free cereals.
o   All unprocessed nuts.

The importance of the descriptions "unprocessed" and "simple" is that during processing, manufacturers frequently add gluten-containing substances for a number of food technology reasons. Unfortunately, gluten turns out to be a very useful ingredient in manufacturing.

If food is processed, it may contain gluten

Which cereals / grains are gluten-free?

The following is the list of gluten-free grains. However, yet again if these are processed, you have to check that they remain gluten-free.

o   Rice (flour, cakes, biscuits, pasta, bran, puffs, crackers).
o   MaizeCorn (flour cornmeal, puffs, pasta, crackers).
o   Sago, tapioca.
o   Buckwheat flour (buckwheat is not wheat).
o   Legumes – soy, lentils (whole, flour or sprouts).
o   Potato – flour.
o   Sorghum.
o   Millet.
and
o   Oats – for those who can tolerate them.

Oat is a cereal that each individual will have to work out if it is okay for themselves. Most gluten-sensitive people can tolerate oats very well (see Chapter 1).

Which foods do I have to avoid?

This is a short list! You need to avoid all foods made from:
o   Wheat
o   Rye
o   Barley

To expand a little more on this:

o   Flour from any of these gluten-containing grains.
o   Products made from such flour (e.g. pasta, bread, cakes, rusks, crackers, biscuits, crumpets, bagels, pancakes, pikelets, cookies and muffins).
o   Malt and malt vinegar.
o   Any food that contains added gluten.

These are the simple rules. When you start to buy processed foods (packets and cans), then you can refer to the long lists of specific brand names of gluten-free products. For New Zealand, this information is on the website: www.mfd.co.nz. For a more comprehensive web addresses visit www.doctorgluten.com.

The answers to the following questions should help clarify some of the more subtle gluten-free issues.

How is wheat starch made?
Wheat-grain (and therefore, wheat-flour) is made up mostly of starch granules: about 75% of grain is starch. Starch is the carbohydrate or sugary part of the grain.

When wheat starch is refined, small amounts of gluten protein will stick to the surface of the starch granules. The amount of gluten that remains stuck in the starch depends on the washing method and how many times the granules are washed. It is possible to manufacture wheat starch that is very low in surface gluten proteins.

Starch might contain gluten

If a food contains starch, will it also contain gluten?
Starch is the white substance in grains and root vegetables. It is where the plant stores its sugars. So it depends upon from where the starch is derived as to whether or not it contains gluten. If it is gluten-free, then you can eat it.

Starch that comes from the root vegetables such as potatoes, parsnip, carrot and kumura is fine. It does not contain gluten. Starch that is made from corn and rice is also free of gluten. Here is the important bit: starches (including modified starch and thickeners) that are made from the gluten-containing grains (wheat, rye and barley) *will* contain traces of gluten. This includes the "1400 range" of food thickeners and they are usually described in the ingredient list as – "thickener" or "modified starch". These types of starches are produced from a variety of grains, including wheat.

The problem stems from the incomplete processing of these cereal starches, and the fact that the source of starch is rarely noted in the ingredient list. Therefore, this whole group of modified starch thickeners is best avoided *unless* the starch source is clearly stated. Miazecorn starch is okay.

What is a maltodextrin?

Maltodextrin is just another word for starch. The word is derived from "maltose" (a sugar disaccharide made up from two glucose molecules) and "dextrin" which is a string of glucose molecules. A maltodextrin is a long chain of maltose molecules – that is starch.

Maltodextrin is a name for starch

So, "maltodextrin" is a technical term for starch. It can be refined from a number of grain sources. Some maltodextrins do not contain gluten (derived from potato, maize cornstarch or rice), whilst maltodextrins derived from the gluten-grains (wheat, rye and barley) *do* contain traces of gluten.

The real question is how much maltodextrin can you consume when on a gluten-free diet. The answer is: "as little as practicable." Some people can take small amounts because the quantity of gluten in these additives is tiny. However, other people are so sensitive that they experience unpleasant symptoms with just a trace. You have to work it out yourself.

Do any food additives contain gluten?

Yes! Many food additives are made from gluten containing grains.

o   Amylases: # 1100 – these enzymes may have been produced from malted cereals and therefore may contain traces of gluten. They are commonly used in commercial breads.
o   Glutamates: #620, 621, 622, 623, 624, 625 – they are generally gluten-free. But because some may be derived from wheat, you are best to avoid them.
o   Starch: #1400 range (see previous).
o   Maltodextrin – if derived from wheat (see previous).
o   Malt extract.
o   Vinegar – if malt based.
o   Soy sauce – if wheat based.
o   HVP – Hydrolysed Vegetable Protein.
o   HPP – Hydrolysed Plant Protein.

Many food additives contain gluten

What does hidden gluten mean?

Hidden gluten is the term used to describe possible sources of gluten that you have not yet thought about. Also called unsuspected gluten. Some people are so sensitive to gluten that even the most tiny amounts can upset them. It can be surprising where gluten is found.

Unlisted gluten

The gluten content of some foods is not always listed. That is because small amounts are not required to be put on the list of ingredients. Often, products may list only the main ingredients.

Imported foods may contain unlisted gluten. Food labelling requirements vary from country to country. There are different levels of gluten label requirements in Europe (allows less than 0.02% to denote gluten-free) compared to Australia (allows less than 0.003%). So it is important to check the country of origin. In many parts of the world there is no legislation on labelling of gluten-free foods.

Unlisted gluten can be a problem

The Revised Standard for Gluten-Free Foods states that foods made from naturally gluten-free ingredients should not contain more that 20 parts per million (ppm). Whilst foods made from ingredients that contain gluten (wheat barley and rye) should not contain more than 100 ppm.

Contamination with gluten

When foods are manufactured using the same machinery that has been previously used to make other gluten containing food – then these foods may accidentally contain gluten. This is also called "cross-over" contamination. This is seen in the oats problem.

To commercially prepare gluten-free food, the whole machinery system needs to be gluten-free. Otherwise you can get this cross-over contamination.

People in the hospitality industry are naturally more focused on running their business than concerned about your diet. They do not necessarily have the drive to ensure that their foods are completely free of gluten. Also, they might not understand some of these more subtle ways that gluten can get into your food. Be aware when eating out.

Contamination from cooking in oil and water

If foods are cooked in oil which has been used for deep frying other food such as battered fish – then it may contain gluten.

If foods are boiled in water which has been used for pasta – then it may contain gluten. Food contamination can also occur on grills, breadboards, knives and in tins.

Make-up, medicines, stationery

Some lipsticks and toothpastes contain gluten.
Some medicines and supplements contain gluten.
Glue on some envelopes may contain gluten.

Gluten can be found in a lot of products

Is a gluten-free diet harmful?

No! A gluten-free diet is not harmful. In fact, in my opinion, a gluten-free diet is usually a healthier diet than an unrestricted one. This is because a large amount of fast-foods and empty-calorie foods must be eliminated.

People on a gluten-free diet very quickly learn a lot about food. They are, therefore, in a strong position to make better food choices than the uneducated.

On a gluten-free diet there is less scope for over eating. There is usually less sugar in the diet and, therefore, less obesity. A gluten-free diet is actually a fantastic diet, because you cannot have all those things that are so bad for your heart.

Gluten-free children are more likely to eat lots of fruit and vegetables, eat more protein, and have lower amounts of carbohydrate in their diet.

If you want to feel bouncy and full of energy, then you do not want to fill yourself up with gluten containing foodstuffs – they will just weigh you down.

Do you get more sensitive to gluten?
Yes, it is common to become more sensitive to gluten when you go onto a gluten-free diet. When people first eliminate gluten from their diet, many become incredibly sensitive to gluten.

Previously, they had been eating a normal diet with gluten and feeling a little unwell. But subsequently, when gluten-free, even the tiniest amount of gluten might now spark off a dramatic reaction. This increased sensitivity tends to diminish as the years go by.

How strict does my gluten-free diet need to be?
This is a tricky question to answer. The glib answer is to be as gluten-free as you can possibly achieve. This is probably too extreme for some. However, very small amounts of gluten (one gram per day) are enough to cause sustained bowel damage if you have coeliac disease.

For those with an elevated tTG and an abnormal biopsy, then my advice is to be as strict as possible, lifelong.

Be as strict as you can

However, with gluten-sensitivity, without bowel damage, perhaps a less stringent standard is acceptable. In this regard we are talking about the traces of gluten found in some maltodextrins which many people can consume without experiencing any symptoms.

This is the area of controversy about whether some processed foods, like cornflakes and rice bubbles, can be allowed. They often contain small amounts of malt or maltodextrins. With present knowledge, how strict you are will depend upon whether you develop symptoms. If you do get symptoms with tiny amounts of gluten, then do not eat them. If you do not get symptoms, then there is no evidence that it will cause you ongoing damage in the future. Nobody knows the full answer to this yet.

One way to check for on-going affects is to repeat the anti-gliadin antibody tests every year or so. On a strict gluten-free diet, these antibody levels will fall to normal levels within about twelve months. To be on the safe side, keep your gluten intake to the absolute minimum.

What about lactose intolerance?

Lactose intolerance is the inability to digest lactose. Lactose is the sugar that is found in human breastmilk and mammalian milks, including cow's milk and goat's milk. *Lactase* is the name of the gut enzyme that breaks it down to absorb it.

Lactose is the sugar in milk

Lactose intolerance means that the sugar in milk (lactose) is not digested properly by the small intestine. The villi, that line your small intestine, produce this *lactase* enzyme. This enzyme breaks down the lactose sugar into its two component molecules: glucose and galactose. Lactose cannot be absorbed without it first being broken down into these smaller sugars. When the villi in the mucosa of your gut are damaged because of gluten toxicity, then the lactase does not get produced. The result of this is that the lactose passes through your small intestine into your large bowel.

If the lactose gets through to your large bowel, it is rapidly fermented by the bugs in your colon. This produces gas and attracts water into your bowel motions. The result is uncomfortable. The fermented gas gives you bloating and all of the extra water gives you loose motions.

Thus, if you eat a lot of lactose (milk and yoghurt), then a lot of lactose will be fermented and you will get explosive diarrhoea, abdominal distension and cramp.

In most people with coeliac disease, the associated lactose intolerance is totally reversible when they go onto a gluten-free diet. After a few weeks or months, the villi are usually restored, their function becomes normal and lactase can be manufactured again. Therefore, you would again tolerate lactose in your diet.

Gut damage can cause lactose malbasorption

I advise that milky products are slowly introduced after 4–8 weeks on a gluten-free diet. In children, the gut heals much more rapidly than in adults.

In adults it may take several months before lactose will be tolerated. Even then there may be still a degree of lactose intolerance.

Does milk allergy get better on gluten-free?
No. Milk allergy is different to lactose intolerance. When you have a milk allergy, you are reacting to the protein in the milk (not the lactose). Unfortunately, the allergy is likely to persist, despite going on a gluten-free diet.

What about Lactobacillus Acidophilus?

Your large bowel (colon) is teeming with bacteria. They are essential for your good health. The most important of these bacteria are the two species:

o   Lactobacillus acidophilus
o   Bifidobacteria species

These are the "good bugs" in your gut. They help both you and your large bowel keep healthy. These are the bugs that do some of the fermenting of the lactose, if it gets through to your colon.

The technical name for these good bugs is "probiotics". They digest the waste material that comes through your small intestine. They especially digest the fibre content of your food. This fermentation process produces gas. So, if you eat a very fibrous food like beans (that has a sugary fibre), then you will make a large amount of rectal gas. This can be the cause of the abdominal bloating and distension.

Fermentation of malabsorbed food causes bloating

A crucial feature of these probiotics is that they produce breakdown metabolites that help feed the mucosa of your colon (the skin of your large intestine). This mechanism also has a magical immunological effect that is a very important part of your immune system.

With the right bugs in your gut (Lactobacillus Acidophilus and the bifidobacteria species) your immune function will improve. This effect has been shown to reduce allergic reactions and help repair any gut dysfunction.

These bugs should be in your colon in high amounts. When you do not digest your food properly, because of coeliac disease or gluten-sensitivity, then the malabsorbed food comes through and feeds these bacteria. However, because inappropriate nutrients have now entered the large bowel, this will encourage the growth of the "wrong" species of bacteria.

Probiotics stimulate your immune function

Some of these "wrong" bacteria can produce a lot more gas in your gut. This gives you a big bloated tummy and makes you feel very uncomfortable, passing embarrassing wind. Sometimes it is necessary to give a bowel antibiotic (usually metronidazole) to kill off some of these excess bacteria. If this is done, it is essential to go onto a high-quality L. Acidophilus replacement supplement.

Once you go gluten-free, you should expect your symptoms to disappear within several weeks to months. How quickly your large bowel recovers has a lot to do with the species of bugs in your gut. If you do not have the right bugs in your gut, then you will continue to have symptoms for some time.

Also, unless your gut function returns to normal, you are not going to get your immune function restored back to normal. Taking Acidophilus every day will help.

Look after the bugs in your gut

Do you need mineral-vitamin supplements?

Yes, I believe that you do need to take a mineral-vitamin supplement to speed your recovery. There are vast numbers of studies that report the many benefits of additional minerals and vitamins to your diet.

In the context of being gluten-sensitive, the gut has not been working properly. That means the absorption of foods, minerals and vitamins has been suboptimal. The consequence is that slowly, but surely, deficiencies of many of your key micro-nutrients will develop.

The outcome can be iron deficiency, other mineral deficiency, anaemia, osteoporosis, vitamin deficiency, immuno-deficiencies and neurological damage. Instead of waiting for these manifestations to occur, it would be wise to reverse these shortfalls *immediately* – before they show up as clinical problems.

I recommend that everyone who is gluten-sensitive, when going gluten-free, should take a high quality mineral-vitamin supplement for at least six months. There is a lot of data that recommends lifetime supplementation if you want to ensure robust health and longevity.

Are all multivitamin supplements the same?

No. Definitely not. Many supplements are of poor quality and their bio-availability is questionable. That means it is very important, that once you have swallowed your supplements, that they actually get absorbed by your gut in a way that your body can readily use them.

Many supplements do not have adequate amounts of selenium in them. It is important to get the right mix of these vitamins and minerals, every day.

8. What is the gluten-sensitive data?

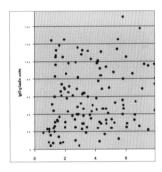

Gluten-sensitive children diagnosed by IgG-gliadin

This chapter presents data which clearly demonstrates that about one-in-ten of the population is gluten-sensitive. This can be readily identified by the IgG-gliadin blood test. These people dramatically respond to a gluten-free diet, but they do not have coeliac disease.

Background

To date, the development of blood tests has exclusively focused on making an accurate diagnosis of coeliac disease.

In the context of this book, the term coeliac disease is confined to those people who have *abnormal* small bowel in association with an appropriate clinical presentation. This gut damage is caused by gluten in genetically susceptible people. This gut damage is detected by looking at a piece of tissue under the microscope (this is called *histology*). This tissue is obtained by upper gastrointestinal endoscopy.

IgG-gliadin measures a reaction to gluten

Two categories of blood test have been developed:
1) tests that detect antibodies to *gliadin* (or gluten).
2) tests that detect small bowel *tissue* damage.

These two tests measure very different things. In coeliac disease, *both* tests are usually positive. The details about these blood tests are given in Chapter 5.

Traditionally, the reliability of blood tests has been determined by the degree of tissue damage that is seen in the small bowel biopsy. If any potential test is not consistently found to be associated with *small bowel damage*, then that test will declared "non-specific".

Under these circumstances, it has been found that the gluten antibody, IgG-gliadin, is a *poor* predictor of coeliac disease. By contrast, the tissue antibody, tissue transglutaminase (tTG) is a *very good* predictor of coeliac disease. Subsequently, the medical world is starting to discard IgG-gliadin testing. I believe that this is throwing the baby out with the bath water. In my clinical practice I have found that IgG-gliadin is an extremely valuable test.

IgG-gliadin detects people who are *gluten-sensitive*.

Although IgG-gliadin does *not* reliably identify coeliac disease, nevertheless, it *does* detect people who are *gluten-sensitive*. The purpose of this chapter is to present the data on this newly recognised clinical entity: gluten-sensitivity. In my opinion, this data validates the measurement of IgG-gliadin in appropriate people. But first, it is important to understand the restrictive thinking that is a consequence of the "sequence effect."

The sequence effect

As told earlier, the story of coeliac disease began 120 years ago. It was just over 50 years ago that gluten toxicity was recognised to be the cause of this disease. It was 40 years ago that techniques were developed to obtain small pieces of bowel tissue for examination (the "small bowel biopsy"). But, the development of the antibody blood tests is relatively recent. The first blood tests became available only about 20 years ago.

Tests that measure IgG-gliadin have been widely available for only 10 years. The tissue transglutaminase (tTG) antibody test has been in use for only about 5 years.

Throughout all this time, the "sequence effect" has been in operation. The sequence effect describes that phenomenon that complex information and knowledge initially comes to us bit by bit: in a sequence. It has been shown that the sequence in which discoveries are made has a big influence on future thinking.

The sequence of information influences thinking

What has gluten got to do with the sequence effect? Well, this sequence effect has misled the medical community into thinking that gluten-sensitivity is a *gut* disease. It works like this: there has been over a hundred years of thinking that coeliac disease is *only* a gut disease. Consequently, when the blood tests became available, people could only think in terms of the gut. But, if these blood tests had been developed *first*, then the whole idea of gluten-sensitivity would have developed in another direction. A different perspective would have been possible because the medical research system would not have been thinking "gut".

Blinkered eyes

Unfortunately, the relevance of the IgG-gliadin blood test has been examined with blinkered eyes. This narrow focus has led to the search for a diagnostic test for coeliac disease without stopping to think about what the gluten blood tests really mean in the wider clinical picture. The tTG test is highly predictive for coeliac disease. But the IgG-gliadin test is not.

Unknowingly, operating under the sequence effect, the logic has been to discard the IgG-gliadin test in favour of tTG. However, this is like throwing the baby out with the bath water. In my experience, the IgG-gliadin is an extremely valuable test.

The habitual words that are used by medics to explain away any meaning of a positive IgG-gliadin is to call it a "non-specific" test. However, this is a ridiculous thing to say because this test in fact measures a *very specific* immunological reaction to gluten.

IgG-gliadin test is a valuable and specific test

The problem is that no one has yet systematically evaluated the clinical meaning of this test. This is the objective of this study. I will describe the gluten-sensitive picture and give extensive data to back this up.

The gluten-sensitive picture

These people who are gluten-sensitive (children and adults) have a *clinical* reaction to gluten, but they *do not* have small bowel mucosa damage. Those with classical coeliac disease have been excluded.

Their symptoms are similar to those with coeliac disease. They have an impressive clinical response to a gluten-free diet. They have high levels of IgG-gliadin but low levels of tTG. Their IgA-gliadin is often slightly elevated. Their endoscopy findings do not show small bowel damage but many show oesophagitis, gastritis or low disaccharidase levels.

So, these patients are similar in all respects to those with coeliac disease except that they have normal bowel histology. Some of these people will have "potential" or "latent" coeliac disease (that means that as time progresses, they will eventually develop the small bowel tissue damage and elevated tTG levels). However, most will not progress along this path to coeliac disease. There is frequently a strong family history. This condition is very much more common than coeliac disease.

To summarise, people who are "gluten-sensitive" have:
o   a wide variety of symptoms that are the same as those associated with coeliac disease.
o   elevated IgG-gliadin antibodies.
o   sometimes elevated IgA-gliadin antibodies.
o   normal levels of tTG antibody.
o   normal small bowel tissue.
o   often a family history of similar illness.
o   impressive clinical responses to a gluten-free diet.

A mixed group

The diagnosis "gluten-sensitive" is made if there is a combination of high IgG-gliadin levels and a clinical response to a gluten-free diet, in the absence of small bowel damage. The consequence of this verdict is that this group will necessarily include two main groups of people:

1. Those who are gluten-sensitive, who do not have the propensity to develop small bowel tissue damage, but who are clinically intolerant to gluten (in my experience, this group is less likely to have the coeliac HLA types).

2. Those with early coeliac disease, but who are yet to manifest any small bowel tissue damage. These are the so-called potential or latent coeliacs (they can be identified by measuring their HLA status).

The next section presents the study design and the clinical data.

Study design

This study was a clinical audit. All patient data was extracted retrospectively. All patients were seen in my children's gastroenterology and allergy clinic in Christchurch, New Zealand.

The purpose of this audit is to demonstrate that there are large numbers of children who are extremely sensitive to gluten in their diet but *do not* have coeliac disease.

IgG-gliadin levels are crucial to make the diagnosis

Blood tests were requested for all children with chronic gut symptoms or who were suspected of having coeliac disease, iron deficiency or any immunological problems. Many children had two or more blood tests over the years of their follow up. The results of blood tests for: IgG-gliadin; IgA-gliadin; tissue transglutaminase (tTG); and endomesial antibodies (EMA) are reported.

The study children

Children who were included in this study met the following criteria:
o   Had one or more blood tests for IgG-gliadin and tTG (or EMA).
o   Their last blood test was between the years 2000–2004.
o   They had been eating gluten prior to the blood test.
o   There was clinical follow-up information available.

A total of 291 children were included. Their average age was 4.6 years (ranging from 8 months to 16 years old). Their symptoms are listed in the table in order of the frequency. In total, 207 (71%) had some sort of gut symptoms. Nearly half experienced abdominal pain.

Symptoms	Number (n=291)	Percent (%)
Abdominal pain	136	47
Eczema	91	31
Poor weight	86	30
Reflux (GORD*)	82	28
Diarrhoea	72	25
Irritable	65	22
Run down	61	21
Poor height	49	17
Pot tummy	43	15
Tired/lethargy	42	14
Constipation	39	13
Poor sleep	36	12
Hyperactive	31	11
Vomiting	26	9
Headache	13	4

*(GORD = Gastro Oesophageal Reflux Disease)
The total number of patients does not equal the sum of the symptoms described because most of these children had a combination of problems.

Analysis and results

The focus of this study was to validate the *clinical* value of the IgG-gliadin test. Therefore, the data is presented in the following way:

1. First, the total group was examined for the blood test results (291 children).
2. Then, the biopsy data was examined to determine who had coeliac disease (14 children).
3. Next, the clinical features of all the other children who had a clinical response to a gluten-free diet were described (123 children).
4. Finally, there was a group of children who are still under review as their gluten status is not yet decided (62 children).

1) IgG-gliadin & tTG antibodies for all children

The IgG-gliadin and the tTG antibodies for all 291 children were examined by age to show the overall picture of the blood test results.

IgG-gliadin levels

The focus of this study is on the clinical value of IgG-gliadin in diagnosing children who are gluten-sensitive. The question is "What do these blood tests mean in the clinical context?" To give the size of the problem, all IgG-gliadin test results are shown in *Figure 1.*

72% of the children had high IgG-gliadin

A raised IgG-gliadin level is more than 20 units (shown by the heavy line). The striking feature about this graph is the very large proportion of children with raised IgG-gliadin levels. Even by one year of age there are children with very high IgG-gliadin

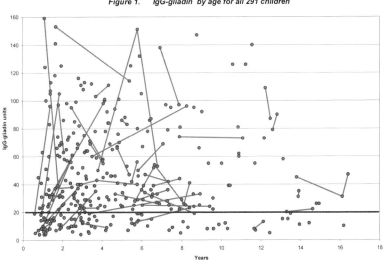

Figure 1.   IgG-gliadin by age for all 291 children

levels. There were 356 IgG-gliadin blood tests, of which 255 (72 %) were above the "normal" limits of 0–20 units. The lines join up children who had more than one set of blood tests. There are some rapidly rising IgG-gliadin levels in the first years of life. Once up, the levels appear to remain high whilst the child continues to eat gluten. However, the blood tests have not been adjusted for the amounts of gluten being eaten. There is a tendency for gluten-sensitive children to spontaneously remove gluten from their diet: it makes them feel unwell. This might be the explanation for some of the falling levels that you can see.

IgA-gliadin

IgA-gliadin levels for all of these 291 children are shown in *Figure 2*. There were 355 blood tests of which 28 (8%) children had elevated levels (normal levels less than 15 units). I have not found that the IgA-gliadin test contributes much to the diagnosis. However, it gives more suspicion that there could be a significant reaction to gluten.

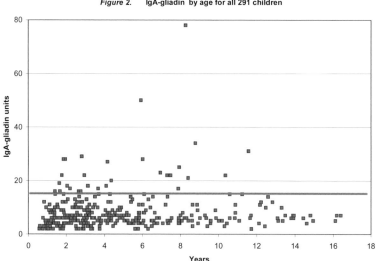

Figure 2.   IgA-gliadin by age for all 291 children

tTG levels

The tTG levels for all children are shown in *Figure 3*. The tTG levels were much less scattered with a few high measurements. However, the vast majority of tTG levels were normal (less than 20 units).

There were 285 tTG blood tests, of which only 18 (6 %) were above the "normal" limit. I recommend an endoscopy for all those with a high tTG – however, not everyone accepts. The 18 positive tTG tests came from 17 patients, of whom 11 had a small bowel biopsy. All but one of these biopsy results had some abnormality. This demonstrates the value of the tTG test: which is highly reliable at identifying tissue damage in people over five years of age.

EMA testing also looks for tissue damage. In these children, 91 had an EMA test of which 12 (13%) were positive. Thus, the total "tissue" antibody tests were positive in 30 of 376 (8%) tests.

Figure 3. tTG by age for all 291 children

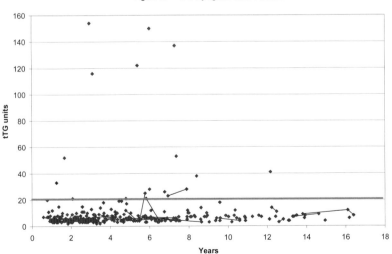

113

The conclusion from these three graphs is that IgG-gliadin is very frequently high in this group of patients, but few have evidence of tissue damage. This means that the IgG-gliadin test tells much more about gluten-sensitivity than it does about gut damage.

2) The value of small bowel biopsy

Without first excluding classic coeliac disease, the remainder of the data becomes irrelevant to us. We have to find out who actually does have small bowel damage.

Endoscopy

The endoscopy procedure is a crucial investigation to determine if and where there is tissue damage or poor function. The term "villus atrophy" is used to describe the classical biopsy changes seen in coeliac disease. The diagnosis of coeliac disease cannot be definitively made in the absence of small bowel damage (although biopsy is not always reliable).

Importantly, additional information can be gained from endoscopy by sampling tissue in the oesophagus and in the stomach. Also, the function of the small bowel can also be assessed by measuring the enzyme activity of the disaccharidases (lactase, maltase and sucrase) in small bowel tissue. The guidelines that I use to determine which children should undergo a small bowel biopsy are if they have any of these four features:

o   Elevated tTG or EMA antibodies.
o   Elevated IgA-gliadin levels (usually IgG gliadin is also substantially raised).
o   Considerably elevated IgG-gliadin levels with symptoms and no family history.
o   Those failing to thrive (poor growth) without explanation and who have negative coeliac and gluten antibody markers.

(In my experience, the biopsy is nearly always histologically normal in children, over five years of age, who have minor symptoms and who only have moderately elevated IgG-gliadin, with normal tTG).

Biopsy results

There were 75 children (26% of the total 291 children) who had a small bowel biopsy.

Endoscopy is a crucial investigation

The biopsy results of the histology (oesophagus and small bowel) and disaccharidases were categorised into four mutually exclusive groups: normal; coeliac histology; oesophagitis; and low disaccharidases. These results were then compared with their blood tests results. This information is given in the table.

Biopsy result	Number (n=75)	tTG >20 or EMA +ve	IgG-gliadin >20	IgA-gliadin >15
Normal	28	5 (18%)	23 (82%)	4 (14%)
Coeliac histology*	14	8 (62%)#	12 (87%)	4 (29%)
Oesophagitis**	13	3 (23%)	12 (92%)	3 (23%)
Low Disacchs**	20	1 (5%)	19 (95%)	7 (35%)
Total	75	17 (23%)	66 (88%)	18 (24%)

Notes: * Many of the Coeliac histology children also had low
disaccharidases and/or oesophagitis.
** These groups had normal small bowel histology
# only 13 had tTG/EMA test)

115

The main points to be drawn from this data are:
o   Abnormalities were seen in 47 (63%) of these biopsies.
o   There were only 14 children with diagnostic coeliac histology. Of these 14 children, just over half (62%) had an abnormal ttG (or EMA). The probable explanation is the young age of some of these patients. On the other hand, 87% had high IgG-gliadin readings.
o   In all four biopsy categories there was a high percentage of children with elevated IgG-gliadin levels. This is not surprising as this was a criteria for doing the endoscopy. However, over 90% of those with either oesophagitis or low disaccharidases had raised IgG-gliadin levels. This information is shown graphically in *Figures 4 & 5.*

Figure 4 shows the wide range of IgG-gliadin levels that are associated with biopsy categories. The IgG-gliadin was not predictive of coeliac histology.

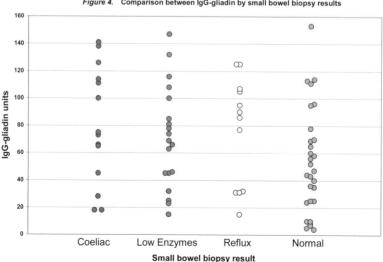

Figure 4. Comparison between IgG-gliadin by small bowel biopsy results

Figure 5, as reported in so many other studies, demonstrates that an elevated tTG level is a good predictor that there will be histological small bowel damage consistent with coeliac disease. The tTG is seldom elevated in the other conditions (it can be raised in chronic liver disease and inflammatory bowel disease).

However, of crucial importance are the four children with coeliac tissue damage but who had low tTG readings. This means that the tTG alone *cannot* be used exclusively to diagnose coeliac disease. If the tTG is negative, then a biopsy is strongly indicated in the presence of symptoms.

The conclusion from this data is that only a few of all these 291 children had coeliac disease: there were only 14 (5%). So what does the positive IgG-gliadin antibody mean for the rest of these children?

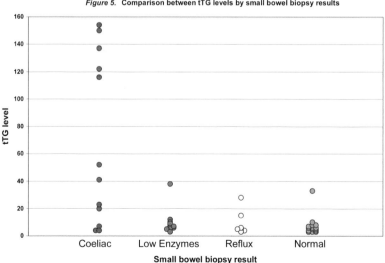

Figure 5. Comparison between tTG levels by small bowel biopsy results

2) The gluten-sensitive group – blood tests

All children who had symptoms and an elevated IgG-gliadin level were put on a gluten-free diet for a trial three-month period. Those who made a good response to the gluten-free diet were called "gluten-sensitive". Of course, the 14 children with coeliac disease were excluded from this group (however, they also went gluten-free!).

IgG-gliadin levels

Figure 6 shows the IgG-gliadin blood results of this group of 123 children who were diagnosed as *gluten-sensitive*. There is a wide range of IgG-gliadin levels. They were mostly above 20 units. However, there are 9 children who had "normal" levels who nevertheless responded to a gluten-free diet. These children were often only eating very small amounts of gluten and were the siblings of families already on gluten-free programmes. The parents discovered that their child was symptomatically much

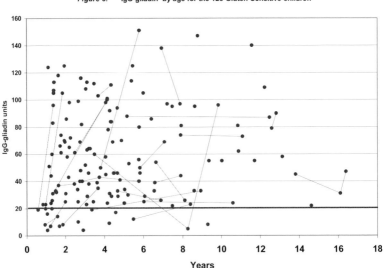

Figure 6. IgG-gliadin by age for the 123 Gluten-Sensitive children

improved off gluten. This demonstrates that a positive IgG-gliadin is not a foolproof method of determining all of those children who will respond to a gluten-free diet. The lines join repeated measurements.

A number of these children have been followed for over six years with their blood tests repeated every two years. Gluten-sensitivity had been suspected but not acted upon because their levels of IgG-gliadin were just hovering around the upper "normal" range. Eventually they went gluten-free with dramatic clinical responses. The lesson from this is that the absolute level of IgG-gliadin is not a sure-fire indicator. Clinical suspicion is needed as well.

ttG and gluten-sensitive

Figure 7 shows the ttG levels for these 123 gluten-sensitive children. They are mostly below 20 units (that is "normal"). Three who had a positive ttG had a normal small bowel biopsy: this excluded them from the definitive coeliac group. However, it is very likely that in the years to come, these children will

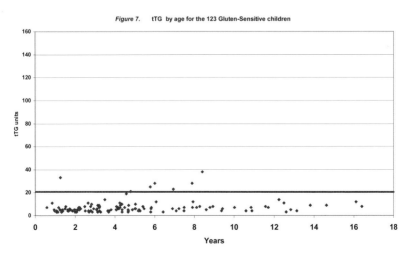

Figure 7. ttG by age for the 123 Gluten-Sensitive children

develop coeliac disease if they are left on gluten. Another three declined biopsy and went gluten-free. They might have coeliac disease. This underscores the difficulty of making a distinction between gluten-sensitive and coeliac disease. This imprecision is because these conditions evolve with age when there is continued gluten exposure. Current thinking is that most children with an elevated tTG test will eventually develop full-blown coeliac disease if left on gluten. A way to distinguish these children is to measure their HLA type.

Relationship with small bowel biopsy

Because of the never-ending question of the small bowel biopsy, I now present the biopsy findings of these *gluten-sensitive* children. There were 55 (45%) who had a small bowel biopsy. By definition, they all showed normal small bowel tissue (obviously, if the histological was abnormal then these children have already been classified as coeliacs).

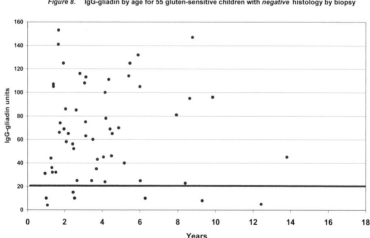

Figure 8. IgG-gliadin by age for 55 gluten-sensitive children with *negative* histology by biopsy

Of this biopsy group, 7 had evidence of oesophagitis and 17 had low disaccharidase enzyme levels. So, there were only 31 with a completely normal biopsy.

There were two children in which their first biopsy was normal, but their second biopsy a few years later showed them to now have developed coeliac disease. Coeliac disease is an evolving condition.

Figure 8 shows the levels of IgG-gliadin for this *negative* biopsy group. Nearly all have high IgG-gliadin levels, but not all. Obviously, a high IgG-gliadin level is not predictive of an abnormal gut.

Figure 9 presents the tTG levels in the small bowel biopsy *negative* group. Only three children had a positive tTG and normal small bowel tissue. This figure emphasises that tTG is not perfect. However, these three children need careful watching. In the future they are very likely to develop coeliac disease.

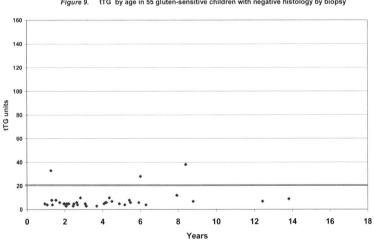

Figure 9. tTG by age in 55 gluten-sensitive children with negative histology by biopsy

3) The gluten-sensitive group – the clinical picture

There have been no previous studies describing the symptoms of gluten-sensitive children. Also there is no information on the relationships between the *clinical symptoms* and IgG-gliadin levels. It has been my policy, over the last five years, to place children on a three-month gluten-free trial if they meet the following criteria:

- o They had clinical symptoms
- o They did not have coeliac disease (as shown by biopsy, if appropriate)
- o They had elevated IgG-gliadin levels.

There were 123 children who made a positive clinical response to a gluten-free diet. These children had a wide range of symptoms. Those who were most unwell usually had multiple symptoms. The symptoms that were experienced by these children are given in the table.

Gluten-sensitivity has wide ranging symptoms

The great majority of these children (84%) presented with gastrointestinal symptoms (my speciality). However, a wide spectrum of other symptoms was encountered. In the "coeliac world" constipation and gastro-oesophageal reflux are considered to be minor symptoms.

However, I found that about a quarter of these gluten-sensitive children had these symptoms. Behaviour disturbances were also very common. Some children presented with behaviour concerns alone, including Attention Deficit Hyperactivity Disorder (ADHD).

Gluten-sensitive symptoms of 123 children

	Number	Percent
Gut symptoms	**101**	**82 %**
Abdominal pain	70	58 %
GORD (reflux)	33	27 %
Diarrhoea	30	24 %
Constipation	24	20 %
Vomiting	18	15 %
Growth concerns	**62**	**50%**
Poor weight	41	33 %
Poor height	21	17 %
Pot tummy	28	23 %
Behaviour concerns	**59**	**48 %**
Irritable	32	26 %
Poor sleep	28	23 %
Tired/lethargy	25	20 %
Hyperactive/defiant	19	15 %
Headache	7	6 %
Allergy/Immune	**56**	**45 %**
Eczema	30	24 %
Run down	23	19 %

The list of symptoms that are experienced by children who are gluten-sensitive includes *all* of the manifestations with which coeliac disease can present. But there are additional symptoms. I would like to make special mention of several of these.

Short stature

Growth concerns were found in half (50%) of these children. These children were often short and thin. Although they did not have coeliac disease, they regained lost ground on a gluten-free diet. They began to eat more and grow again. Any short thin child should be tested for high IgG-gliadin levels. Thus, this short stature might not be primarily a malabsorption problem.

Run-down

Many children (19%) were "run down". This meant that they were catching every illness going around and always seemed to be unwell. They had a poor appetite and they were frequently on antibiotics. On a gluten-free diet they picked up, ate more and regained their health. Frequently, these children had low iron stores.

Pot tummy

A protuberant abdomen, or "pot tummy", is a common sign for being gluten-sensitive. This was seen in nearly a quarter (23%) of these children. This can develop in the first few years and is very persistent. It will not settle until they go gluten-free. This is due to increased fermentation of food in their bowel due to a combination of slower gut motility, malabsorption, low muscle tone, and different gut bacteria. Many of these children are also short and thin.

Gastro-oesophageal reflux Disease (GORD)

Over a quarter (27%) had GORD. This shows up as crying, vomiting and regurgitation in an infant and epigastric pain and belching in older children. Many of these children required acid-suppression medication (such as ranitidine or omeprazole) until they went gluten-free. I now investigate all GORD children for gluten antibodies if they are still needing acid suppression medication past 18 months of age. The majority of these children turn out to be gluten-sensitive.

Constipation

This is major problem for some of these children. A fifth (20%) were affected. Some had battled with chronic constipation for years and years – all of their childhood. Their constipation was resistant to all normal therapies. However, on going gluten-free, their constipation problems vanished. It might take several months because it takes time for the colon and rectal tone to be re-established and their habits of a lifetime to change.

Hyperactivity

Significant brain disturbance is a very common feature in children who are gluten-sensitive. In this audit, irritability was seen in 27% and hyperactivity or defiant behaviour in 15%. This can be the predominant symptom. A number of children presented with a diagnosis of ADHD. Their symptoms completely settled on a gluten-free diet and they became normal loveable children again. In this audit I did not include the children with Autism who also experienced benefits on a gluten-free diet.

Cow's milk allergy and multiple food allergy

Food allergy was found in 38 (31%) children which included cow's milk allergy, seen in 25 (21%). This caused a number of different symptoms. In some, it was associated with GORD, diarrhoea or constipation. In others there was an immediate allergic reaction associated with positive skin prick tests and eczema. It becomes a huge challenge to overcome when your child reacts to multiple foods (especially, cow's milk, egg, peanut and sometimes soy) and then in addition, gets diagnosed as gluten-sensitive. This makes going gluten-free much more difficult. However, the children are usually so much better that the parents are pleased to have a solution to their child's problems.

Eczema

A quarter of these children (24%) had eczema. Many of these children also had allergies to other foods (especially cow's milk, egg and peanut).

Amazing responses to gluten-free diets

These children were taken off gluten for a three month's trial. Some of their parents' impressions are as follows.

Verbatim comments from parents after three months of gluten-free
Best he has ever been
Great – been on very little gluten
Huge improvement
Excellent
Much happier – good attitude change
Improved – much better
Happy and more energy within days
Excellent growth. Great progress
Very much better
Greatly helped behaviour
Fantastic improvement. Different child
Dramatic response, happy again
Very sensitive to gluten
Great on gluten free
Not as many upset stomachs – better
Fantastic
A bit better
Wonderful improvement
Best she has been
A lot better off gluten
Slight improvement but not dramatic
Seems to be doing better.
Took a while to improve
Very happy with progress! Flourishing
Happier, coming off reflux medication
Good response
More energy
Much more healthy
More energy, normal bowels at last
Much better health, now sleeping. A remarkable improvement
Very much better
Huge improvement
Happier, more attentive and sleeping through the night

Dramatically better
Growing again. Good health
Skin improved off gluten
Very much improved. Very sensitive to gluten
Behaviour much better
Happy and flat tummy. We are over the moon
Much better – no more sore tummies
Symptoms disappeared
He feels good again. All symptoms disappeared
Very much better. Symptoms gone away
Improved mood, energy, and health.
Much better
A lot better. Happy again
Improving fast. Big difference
More energy, stopping scratching – I cannot believe it
A bit better. Now growing
Much better. Improved behaviour
Doing very well
Much better. Less irritable
Very good, tummy much better
More energetic
Happier, more energy
A new child. Perked up and thriving
Much better – fantastic
Improved significantly
No pain and getting better
Very pleased with progress
Best she has ever been
After two months she was wonderful and energetic
Happier and lots of energy
Full of energy. Good on the diet
Asking for food for the first time. No pain!!
Fantastic. Huge improvement in everything
Phenomenal difference
Big difference
Good benefit – much better
Better
Great response. Been really good
Slowly getting better. Great after six months

Better
Wonderful change in behaviour and temperament
Much better!
Sleeping better and so much happier
Made a huge improvement
Picked up well. Great health
Doing very well. Much, much better
Excellent. Very sensitive to gluten
Wonderful – a miracle. Lots of energy and bowels normal
Improved considerably, much better
An amazing result
Much better now
Good! Happier. Back to normal
Changed her life. Huge difference
Huge improvement
Really good. A different girl

These comments surely speak for themselves. Nearly all children had impressive improvements. As more time went by, these children became more and more healthy, energetic and happy. The whole family benefited. Frequently, siblings and parents were also diagnosed as being gluten-sensitive and so the overall wellbeing of the family was hugely improved.

Going gluten-free makes a huge difference

Once these children had gone onto a gluten-free diet, they usually became even more sensitive to gluten. Thus, when they were later exposed to a small amount of gluten, they experienced a much more dramatic adverse reaction. This helped reinforce, for both the child and the parents, the need for them to be on their gluten-free diet. My threshold for putting people on gluten-free diets has become steadily lower as I repeatedly hear these wonderful stories.

What symptoms are caused by gluten?

I have identified four symptom groups: gut, growth, behaviour and allergy/immune. So the next question was: "Is there any relationship between these groups of symptoms and their antibody levels (IgG-gliadin and tTG). This data is given in *Figures 10 and 11.*

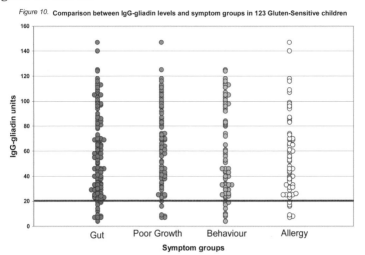

Figure 10. Comparison between IgG-gliadin levels and symptom groups in 123 Gluten-Sensitive children

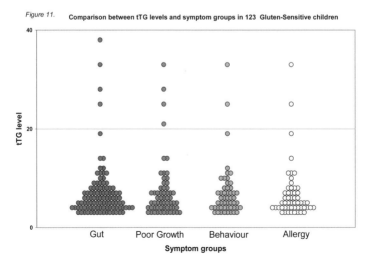

Figure 11. Comparison between tTG levels and symptom groups in 123 Gluten-Sensitive children

The amazing answer to this question was that there were *no* differences between the four symptom groups. All four groups had the same wide range of IgG-gliadin and tTG levels. The gut symptoms *did not* predominate. In all four groups, the great majority of the children had elevated IgG-gliadin antibodies.

Some children had low levels of IgG-gliadin. The explanation is that these children were noted to be gluten-sensitive very early in their life. Therefore, they were only eating very small amounts of gluten at the time of the blood tests. Most of them had a sibling who was already on a gluten-free diet.

The conclusion to draw from this data is that it is very difficult to predict, from just the symptoms, who has high levels of IgG-gliadin. Because the symptom range is extremely wide, the only strategy that works is to do IgG-gliadin blood tests on *everyone* who has persistent troublesome symptoms. Many will be gluten-sensitive.

3) Children who are still under review

Diagnosis is not straight forward

I have a large number of children (62) who are still under review. They have high IgG-gliadin levels but they have few if any symptoms. This group is shown in *Figure 12.* They are often the brothers and sisters of children who have already been diagnosed as coeliac or gluten-sensitive. These children have elevated IgG-gliadin levels but have *not* been put on a gluten-free diet for a number of reasons. I anticipate that many of these children will later be confirmed to be gluten-sensitive. Indeed, that is the pattern that I have already seen. These children with high IgG-gliadin levels, at some time later, often when stressed by an illness, will then develop chronic symptoms. When they eventually go on a gluten-free diet, they recover fully.

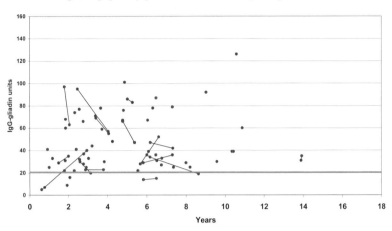

Figure 12 IgG-gliadin by age in 62 children under review for possible gluten-sensitive

Not everyone who is faced with the prospect of going gluten-free will attempt the diet. Particularly, those who are already on restricted diets because of other adverse food reactions. Some of these children have few symptoms, others have no symptoms (family history) and some point-blank refused to give gluten-free a go. These children are therefore still "under review" by me.

As yet I do not know their outcome. However, I believe that they need to be followed carefully. I predict that a few will eventually develop classical coeliac disease; some will have growth failure; some will develop other symptoms; some are likely to remain asymptomatic. In addition, many of the parents are under review! My experience in dealing with the parents of these children is that many of them are also gluten-sensitive. Many of these parents have had chronic tiredness and ill health for decades. Once they go gluten-free they feel alive again.

Discussion

I have presented ample evidence that this clinical picture "gluten-sensitivity" is a very real problem – and a common one. Gluten-sensitivity is *not* coeliac disease. However, I see it as a disease spectrum that *includes* coeliac disease.

The gluten-sensitive idea needs new thinking

In the clinical area of gastroenterology and food allergy, I have shown that elevated levels of IgG-gliadin can be found in the majority of patients. Very few of these patients have coeliac disease (i.e. no small bowel abnormality). So the big question is: "What do these high levels of IgG-gliadin indicate?" Currently, most of these results are being ignored. They are being universally reported as "non-specific" results. This term of "non-specific" is used to say that the test results are not closely related to coeliac disease.

A major shift in thinking

A paradigm shift in thinking is needed. This means that the whole question of adverse reactions to gluten needs to be seen from a different point of view. Up until now, adverse reactions to gluten have been restricted to the entity of coeliac disease: a gut disease with abnormal histology of the small bowel mucosa. This occurs in about one in a hundred people.

Gluten-sensitivity affects one-in-ten

But this can no longer be the case. The condition "gluten-sensitivity" embraces a much wider spectrum of disorders and is perhaps *ten times* more frequent than coeliac disease. That means that one-in-ten people will be affected adversely by gluten.

Ten target organs

In Chapter 3 the diagram that portrays this comprehensive concept of gluten-sensitivity. I believe that there are a large number of different target organs in your body that can each be badly affected by gluten. The small bowel (coeliac disease) is just one of these ten target organs. This is a big list of target organs and symptoms. The clinical picture is so varied. This is why up to now it has not been properly recognised.

Some people are attacked by gluten in one target organ, whilst others are attacked simultaneously in many different places. This explains the wide diversity of illnesses and severity of their symptoms. The reason why various people have different target organs affected is likely to be determined by their genetic make up. This would explain why there are close associations with coeliac disease (small bowel target organ) and certain HLA types (DQ2 and DQ8). On the other hand, these HLA types are not so strongly associated with diseases found at the other target sites.

Small bowel is a minor player

This big picture shows that gluten-sensitivity is much more extensive than just coeliac disease. The gluten focus on coeliac disease has been so narrow that other parts of this picture have gone completely unnoticed. The tTG test has been developed to identify the small bowel damage. It does this very well. However, it furnishes no information about the other potential target organs. Because of the success of detecting coeliac disease by the tTG test, there is a move to scrap IgG-gliadin testing because many doctors consider it to be too unreliable in the context of coeliac disease. This is tantamount to throwing the baby out with the bath water. The IgG-gliadin test is an essential tool to detect the huge numbers of children (and adults) who are sensitive to gluten but do not have the tissue manifestations of coeliac disease.

So how common is gluten-sensitivity?

The recent epidemiologic studies that have been designed for working out how many people have coeliac disease (using tTG and/or biopsy techniques) puts the incidence at around 1-in-100. This means that about 1-in-100 children have, or are developing coeliac disease.

In this clinical audit of my patients, I found just 14 children with "biopsy-proven coeliac disease" and only 18 children with raised tTG levels. However, there were 123 children who were clinically gluten-sensitive. In addition, I am certain that many more children will be added to this number as more are declared gluten-sensitive from the "under review" group.

In my calculations, I have to take into account that I am called "Doctor Gluten" by the community. Therefore, children with more obvious coeliac disease are referred to me. So the numbers of coeliacs are likely to be over-represented.

One-in-ten affected by gluten

From my calculations, I estimate that gluten-sensitivity is *ten times* more common that coeliac disease. This in turn means that at least one person in *ten* (1-in-10) is gluten-sensitive. Are you the one?

1-in-10 people need to be gluten-free

This makes the problem of gluten-sensitivity a gigantic health and social problem. This makes the IgG-gliadin an absolutely essential health tool. In my opinion, *anyone* who has *any* persisting health or brain-related problem should be tested. Some researchers report up to 35% of the western population react adversely to gluten. Already, gluten-free management in the community is becoming a major health industry.

9. How do I learn to eat gluten-free?

What do I need to know for baking gluten-free?

Gluten-free (GF) cooking is certainly more time consuming to start with. It is important to stock up on new GF ingredients for your pantry. It is a good idea to keep gluten-free foods in a special place to avoid confusion and cross-contamination.

Cooking gluten-free can be frustrating because not all of your cooking will turn out perfectly. Give yourself time to practise and to learn how these new ingredients work.

Have a go – it is okay not to be perfect

---

o   The "mix" needs to be wetter for cakes and muffins and drier for biscuits.

o   Instead of cornflour (which can often have wheat in it) use arrowroot, potato flour, or tapioca flour.

o   It is essential to mix any combinations of GF flours thoroughly *before* adding the other ingredients.

o   Chill biscuit mixtures made with GF flours for ½ hour before cutting and baking. They will be easier to handle.

o   Grease tins really well because GF products tend to stick to the tin.

o   GF products are generally better when baked at a slightly *lower* temperature for a longer period of time than the equivalent wheat-based product.

o   Freeze your GF baking in individual servings to keep them fresh and to keep their flavour. You can then thaw each serving, one by one. This technique is great for cakes.

Do you have tips for home bread-maker recipes?

o   When making dough, use warm water. The water temperature will affect how the dough turns out. A water temperature between 18–23^{0}C seems to work well. Experiment to find the texture you like best.

o   Mix the wet and dry ingredients thoroughly with a wooden spoon first. Then transfer the mixture into the bread-maker pan.

o   Once the bread has cooled, slice it all. Either eat it fresh on the same day, or freeze for toasting at a later time.

There are more bread hints in Chapter 10.

How do I convert everyday food to gluten-free?

All Purpose Gluten-Free flour
1 cup *maize* cornflour or arrowroot
2 cups soya flour or chickpea flour
2 cups rice flour
3 cups potato starch flour

Mix well together and store in an airtight container. Use equal cups of this mixture to replace wheat flour in your usual baking recipes. It works best if the recipe is not more than 2 cups of flour. Always bake at a lower temperature for a longer time.

For thickening and for making gravy, use either: maize cornflour, arrowroot or potato flour.

Cornflour may not be made from corn

Note of caution: "corn" is a confusing word. In some parts of the world, this is the word used to denote "wheat". However, in other parts of the world, "corn" it is the word used to describe "maize". So, although cornflour is made from corn, it could come from either wheat or maize, depending on the country! So that is why *maize* cornflour is specified.   Make sure that you find out the source of any cornflour that you use.

Baking powder   To make 1 teaspoon:
use ½ tspn cream of tartar mixed with
¼ tspn bicarbonate of soda.

Cornmeal   Use potato flour, soy flour, millet.

Vinegar   Use lemon juice.

Breadcrumbs can be made by using:
Grated or finely chopped nuts;
or grated potato (or other starchy vegetable);
or grated cauliflower;
or cooked oatmeal;
or crushed and puffed natural breakfast cereal.

What if I have other food allergies?

In addition to gluten, you (or your children) may also be allergic to other foods. Some of these ingredient substitutions may be helpful.

Milk use soy-bean milk;
or rice milk;
or spring water;
or vegetable water;
or fruit juice;
or pureed fruit;
or goat's milk.

Eggs for one egg:
½ tspn baking powder, 2 Tbspns flour, ½ tspn fat;
or 2 Tbspns water, 1 Tbspn oil, 2 Tbspns baking powder;
or 2 Tbspns water, 2 tspns baking powder.

Egg yolk for 1 yolk:
½ tspn baking powder, 2 Tbspns flour.

Egg white for 1 white:
½ Tbspn fat, 1 Tbspn baking powder, 4 Tbspns flour;
or apple or fruit sauce;
or cooked starchy vegetable puree;
or cottage cheese;
or sour milk.

Butter   to make 1 cup:
Egg or gelatine;
or 7/8 cup oil mixed with ½ tspn salt;
or 1 cup animal or poultry fat;
or 1 cup margarine.

Milk and egg allergy are common

Chocolate or cocoa
To make 1 Tablespoon: Use 1 Tbspn carob.
To make 30g: use 3 Tbspns carob or 1½ Tbspns oil.

Do you have breakfast ideas?
o   GF cereal with milk.
o   Fresh fruit and yoghurt and/or GF muesli.
o   GF pancakes, fresh fruit and yoghurt.
o   Toasted GF bread with peanut butter.
o   Fruit smoothie.
o   Eggs, bacon and tomatoes and/or mushrooms.
o   Fried vegetable patties with an egg.
o   Savoury omelette.
o   Oat porridge (if tolerated). Porridge made with oats. Add a Tablespoon of LSA (Linseed, Sunflower and Almond mix) for extra fibre and taste.

Any processed ingredient could contain gluten

Note of caution: Oats are included in some of these ideas. Any oats used must be free of other grain contamination. Each person has to assess their own tolerance to oats.

What can I do for lunch?

Parents usually find ideas for lunch the most challenging. Here are some of the ideas that have been passed on to us.

o   Left-overs (i.e. mince) in taco shells with cheese, tomato, lettuce, avocado.

o   Nacho chips with mince type dip.

o   Stuffed peppers.

o   Left-over mashed potato or kumura mixed with salmon or tuna and fried as patties.

o   Filled baked potatoes, cold or heated.

o   Fried rice – made into a salad.

o   Soups – if at home (no barley).

o   Quiche GF or Pizza GF can be nice cold.

o   Ham roll-ups – use ham with asparagus, cheese, and spring onions rolled up.

o   Salads.

o   Popcorn.

o   Celery stalks – you can fill these with cream cheese.

More lunch ideas

o   Prunes or dates plain or stuffed.

o   GF muffins.

o   Fresh fruit and vegetables.

o   Try this – Gherkins, cheese, olives, dried fruit and nuts with GF dips.

o   Chicken drumsticks.

o   Dried fruit and nuts, raisins, sultanas, prunes, currants, dates, crystallised ginger, dried apricots, peanuts, pumpkin seeds, sunflower seeds.

o   Vegetable sticks, carrot, celery, cucumber, cheese, slices of ham or GF luncheon wrapped around a cube of cheese, orange quarters.

o   Kebabs – celery, GF sausage, cheese, gherkin, tomato.

What help can I get?

Most people need help to get started. Then they can help someone else.

The coeliac support groups are a great source of help, knowledge and encouragement. So join up early.

Your local dietician can help with a range of ideas and give you advice on how to keep a well-rounded diet going.

Your family doctor, paediatrician and gastroenterologist all have important roles in follow-up. Short-term and long-term follow-up is needed to monitor growth, nutrition, bone mineralisation, knowledge, compliance and investigation of family members.

Make meal times fun

We have written a series of books to help you on your road to a healthy gluten-free diet:

o   Going Gluten-Free: How to Get Started.
      The three easy steps to go gluten-free.

o   The Gluten-Free Lunch Book.
      Great ideas for everyone's gluten-free lunches.

o   Gluten-Free Parties and Picnics.
      What to do when your children go out.

    Available from www.doctorgluten.com

10. Do you have some gluten-free recipes?

Disclaimer

Every effort has been taken to ensure that the recipes in this book are correct. As most of these recipes have been contributed, we cannot be held responsible for the results, or for infringement of any copyright. If you see your recipe in this book, we thank you.

Gluten-free recipes

Yes, we do have some gluten-free (GF) recipes. We have asked our gluten-sensitive children and parents to send us their favourite recipes.

These recipes have been collected through various sources by parents and their friends.

A collation of gluten-free recipes from many people

It is impossible to know the origin of all of these recipes that have been handed down from one person to the other over the years. We hope that these will help you with your gluten-free diet.

The most frequent thing that people want to know is how to make a good loaf of bread. You can try out some of the following recipes to see which ones you like the best.

If you can, try and adapt your own recipes by using gluten-free ingredients. Oats are used in some recipes, the reason for this is stated in Chapter 1. Eliminate oats from the recipes if you or your child are intolerant to oats.

Learn to be adventurous and experiment with gluten-free. Ensure that you read the labels of the ingredients you are adding into your baking carefully. Gluten can be in many packet foods.

How do I cook bread?

If you use warm water then the texture of the bread will be nicer.

Once the bread is cooked, let it cool slightly before removing from the pan. You can use an electric knife to slice it while it is still warm or just leave it to cool completely.

Once cooled, slice and eat on the same day or freeze it. As it dries out quite quickly you would need to toast it the next day.

You can buy commercially made gluten-free bread, biscuits, and cakes from many stores, but they tend to be expensive. Once you get used to it, making bread in a home bread-maker is easy and gluten-free baking becomes easier as well.

When you make home-made cakes and slices make a large batch, then when it is cool cut them into pieces, wrap and freeze them so that you will always have baking on hand when you need it and it will be fresh. Gluten-free baking can dry out quite quickly in a short time so putting it in the freezer is best.

Abbreviations:
teaspoon = tspn
Tablespoon = Tbspn
Gluten-free = GF

Bread

Natalie's Brown Bread

Ingredients
Place into a bowl:
2 cups of warm water *or* milk
1¼ tspns yeast
1 Tbspn   brown sugar
3 Tbspns oil
1 egg
approx 500gms GF bread mix;
              or half bread mix and half baking mix
1 heaped Tbspn coarse *maize* cornmeal
1 heaped Tbspn fine *maize* cornmeal *or* rice flour
1 heaped Tbspn ground linseed
1 heaped Tbspn sunflower seeds
1 heaped Tbspn pumpkin seeds [optional]
1 tspn   guar gum.

Method
Mix ingredients gently together.
Scrape the firmish mixture into bread-maker bucket.

Cook on rapid programme with dark crust.
(Bread-makers vary. For some the 'basic' programme gives best results. For others it may work best with the rapid programme. It will need some experimentation).

If bread sinks in centre it may be too moist at the start.

Mock Rye Bread (for bread-maker)

Ingredients
1½ cup   brown rice flour
½ cup   rice bran
½ cup   tapioca flour
½ cup   potato starch flour
1 Tbspn   xanthan (*or* guar) gum
1 Tbspn   caraway seeds
½ tspn   salt
½ cup   dry milk powder (non-instant)
1 Tbspn   cocoa powder
1 tspn   grated orange peel
2 tspn   yeast
2   eggs
3 Tbspns   oil
1 Tbspn   fruit sweetener
2 Tbspns   molasses
1½ cup   water
1 tspn   vinegar.

Method
Follow directions for your particular bread-maker.
Use single rise setting. Best made in small 500g bread machines.

If you have a 1kg machine, you may have better results using the dough setting and baking in a conventional oven (in a 20 x 10 cm pan at 180°C for 50–60 minutes).

Check after first 15 minutes. If top is sufficiently browned, cover with tin foil and continue baking. For ease in slicing, try wrapping in a towel for about 4 hours after it is done baking, and slice with electric knife.
This bread freezes well.

Boston Brown Bread

Ingredients

    1 cup   brown rice flour
    1 cup   white rice flour
    ½ cup potato starch flour
    ½ cup tapioca flour
    ¾ cup popcorn flour *or* ½ cup cornmeal
    3 tspns xanthan gum
    ½ cup buttermilk powder
    1 tspn baking soda
    1½ tspns salt
    2/3 cup raisins
    3 eggs *(or* 1½ tspns Egg Replacer)
    1 tspn vinegar *or* 1 Tbspn dough enhancer
    2/3 cup molasses
    4 Tbspns vegetable oil
    1 1/3 cups water
    2 Tbspns brown sugar
    1 Tbspn   active dried GF yeast.

Method

Blend together the flours, xanthan gum, buttermilk powder, baking soda, (Egg Replacer if used), salt, and raisins.
Beat eggs slightly; add vinegar, molasses, oil, and warm water. Blend thoroughly.

Measure the sugar and yeast.
Place the ingredients in the baking pan of the bread-maker.

Bake on regular bread setting on light or medium heat.

Cakes

Orange and Almond cake

Ingredients

6 medium eggs, separated
2 large oranges
250g caster sugar
225g ground almonds.

Method
Preheat oven to 180°C.
Grease a 23cm round non-stick cake tin.
Line with baking paper.

Put unpeeled whole oranges into a saucepan of water and boil for 2 hours until completely soft.

Remove from saucepan and cool slightly. Cut the oranges and remove the pips. Put the oranges into a food processor and blend with the egg yolks. Then add the sugar and ground almonds a little at a time.
Continue blending until all the ingredients are well combined.

In a separate bowl beat the eggs whites until stiff. Then fold into the orange mixture carefully.

Pour the mixture into the cake tin and cook for 60–70 minutes. Ensure that it is cooked right through.
When cooked remove from oven and allow to cool before turning out.

This cake can be iced with orange-flavoured butter icing or served with yoghurt as a dessert.

Carob Cake

Ingredients – Mix well

    2½ cups GF flour
    2 rounded Tbspn carob powder
    2 rounded tspn baking soda
    1 tspn cinnamon
    1 tspn mixed spice
    1 cup sugar
Choose <u>one</u> of the following options
    2½–3 cups grated carrot *or* courgette
            or grated apple
    2 cups stewed apple
            or mashed banana (or mixed fruits);
    1 cup chopped nuts/seeds mixed
        or raisins
        or dates (chopped and soaked);
        or chopped dried fruit of your choice.

Method
Keep on hand ½ cup liquid (either soak water off dates *or* juice, *or* water).
Mix dry ingredients.
Mix wet ingredients including nuts and fruit.
Mix wet and dry ingredients together well.

If too dry add ½ cup liquid (you often need it – or a bit less or more). If too wet add more flour.

This cake should be a 'firmer' mix. Spoon into a tin lined with baking paper. Cook for 45–60 minutes at 180°C.

Spiced Sponge

Ingredients

4 eggs
2 Tbspns maize cornflour
¾ cup sugar
¼ cup arrowroot
1 tspn mixed spice
1 tspn cinnamon
1 tspn ground ginger
½ tspn bicarbonate of soda
½ tspn cream of tartar
1 Tbspn golden syrup
      or gluten-free rice syrup.

Method
Beat the eggs whites until stiff, add sugar, yolks, spices, cornflour, arrowroot, and last of all the golden syrup.

Bake at 170°C for 25 minutes.
Press lightly with your finger: if the cake springs back then it is cooked.

Note: The spice packet used in this recipe contains (with the proportion in descending order): cinnamon, coriander, nutmeg, pimento, ginger, cassia and cloves

Arrowroot Cake

Ingredients

½ cup butter
¾ cup sugar
2 eggs
1 cup arrowroot
¾ tspn bicarbonate of soda
¾ tspn cream of tartar
3 Tbspns milk
1 tspn cinnamon.

Method
Beat butter and sugar, add yolks of eggs.
Next add arrowroot, bicarbonate of soda and cream of tartar, egg whites, cinnamon and milk.

Bake at 150°C in a ring tin for about 20 minutes.

Ice with whipped cream into which you have folded melted dark chocolate.

Banana Cake

Ingredients

Combine:
    2 cups GF flour mix
    1 tspn salt
    1 tspn cinnamon
    1 tspn   baking soda
    ½ cup   raw sugar.
Stir with a fork.

Measure:
    ½ cup oil and add to dry ingredients.

<u>Do not stir</u>.

Then add
    1 Tbspn vinegar
    3¼ cup (2–3) mashed bananas.

Method
Gently stir until dry ingredients are moist, adding up to ½ cup warm water to make a batter that will drop from a spoon when shaken.

Bake in 18cm square tin (or loaf tin) for 30–35 minutes at 180°C.

Carrot Cake

Ingredients – Mix in big bowl:

2 cups GF flour mix
½ cup raw sugar
1 tspn baking soda
2 tspn cinnamon
1–2 tspn mixed spice
¼ tspn salt
1/3 cup sultanas *or* currants *or* dates
or drained crushed pineapple
or chopped walnuts.

Method
Make a well in the middle of the dry ingredients and add in a cup of oil, 2 cups grated carrot (well packed), and 1 tspn vinegar *or* lemon juice.

Stir until dry ingredients are moist, adding about 2/3 cup water to make a thick batter.

Bake in square tin for about 50 minutes at 180°C.

Date Loaf

Ingredients – Mix together:

1 cup chopped dates
½ cup mixed fruit
½ cup chopped walnuts
¼ cup raw sugar
1¼ cups GF flour mix
1 tspn baking soda.

Add:
1 cup   boiling water
1 tspn vanilla
1 Tbspn oil.

Method
Stir well until all is moistened.
Bake in a loaf tin 40–45 minutes at 180°C.

Pear, Peach or Apple Cake

Ingredients
Mix well:
    2½–3 cups GF flour
    2 rounded tspn GF baking powder
    1 rounded tspn cinnamon
    ½ tspn allspice
    ½ tspn nutmeg
    ¾ cup sugar.

Mix together:
    1 cup raisins or sultanas
    1 cup dates (chopped and soaked or washed in boiling water to soften)
    2½–3 cups bottled pears, apples or peaches
    ½ tspn vanilla (optional but nice).

If needed, ½ cup syrup off apples, pears *or* date soak water, *or* water (you may not need this, because each batch is different due to the type of flour used, amount used, and wetness of stewed fruit).

Method
Mix dry and wet ingredients together.
Add some liquid if feeling too dry, add more flour if too sloppy (it should be a fairly moist mix).
Spoon into a tin lined with baking paper.

Bake at 180°C for 45–60 minutes.

Chocolate Squares

Ingredients

100g dairy-free margarine
1 Tbspn golden syrup
1 cup flour mix
1 cup coconut
1 cup mixed soya rice flakes
1 tspn GF baking powder
1 tspn carob (sieve it necessary)
1 cup sugar.

Method

Melt margarine and syrup together.
Add to rest of ingredients.

Press into sandwich tin and bake at 150°C for 30 minutes.

Ice with carob icing (use carob powder as you would cocoa powder) while warm.

Cut when cold.

Biscuits

Shortbread

Ingredients
100g dairy-free margarine
1 Tbspn golden syrup
1 cup GF flour mix
1 cup mixed rice
1 cup   soy flakes
1 cup coconut
¼ cup raw sugar
1 tspn baking soda

2 Tbspns water.

Method
Melt margarine and syrup together.
Add to dry ingredients with water.

Roll spoonfuls into balls and place on greased oven tray.

Bake at 170°C for 15–20 minutes.

ANZAC Biscuits

Makes 100

Ingredients

2 cups rolled oats
2 cups GF flour
1 cup coconut
1½ cups sugar
250g dairy-free margarine
2 Tbspns golden syrup
1¼ tspn baking soda
½ cup boiling water.

Method
Place rolled oats, flour and coconut in a bowl.
Melt together in medium sized pan the syrup, margarine and sugar.

When sugar is dissolved, mix soda and water and stir into hot margarine mix. Mixture will froth up, so stir immediately into flour. Mix well.

Place small teaspoonfuls on a greased oven tray, allowing room to spread.

Bake at 180°C for 10–15 minutes. Freezes well.

Gingerbread Men

Ingredients

100g dairy-free margarine
100g raw sugar
275g rice flour or GF flour mix
1 tspn bicarbonate of soda
2–3 tspn ground ginger
2½ Tbspns golden syrup
Currants to decorate.

Method
Cream margarine and sugar until very soft. Sieve dry ingredients together then work into creamed mixture.

Add golden syrup to make a dough.

Knead and roll out onto a floured board.
Cut out with gingerbread men cutter.

Place on baking tray, decorate with currant eyes and buttons. Bake for 15 minutes at 190°C.

Allow to cool before removing from baking tray.

Muffins/ small cakes/ slices

Coconut and Ginger Slice

Ingredients

1 cup desiccated coconut
1 1/3 cups shredded coconut
1 cup castor sugar
3 eggs
220g dark chocolate
90g slivered almonds
185g ginger in syrup (including syrup).

Method
Line a 28 x 18cm tin or oven-proof dish with foil.
Melt the chocolate gently on stove, or microwave on high for two minutes. Stir out any remaining lumps.

Spread the chocolate over the foil, going up the sides of the tin about two cms (otherwise the mixture sticks to the foil). Place it in fridge to set. Switch stove on to 175°C.

Beat the eggs, and combine with the other ingredients. You may need to add extra shredded coconut if you use lots of ginger syrup. The more syrup used, the better it tastes.

Spread mixture onto the chocolate.
Bake in centre of oven for half an hour at 175°C.
Turn oven off and leave slice there for a further half hour.

When cool, cut into small pieces.

Fruity Chews (no baking required)

Ingredients

1 cup tofu
2 Tbspns orange juice
1 Tbspn macadamia oil
1 Tbspn lemon juice
1 cup shredded coconut
1 Tbspn raisins, chopped
1 Tbspn prunes, chopped
1 Tbspn almonds, chopped
½ tspn mixed spice
grated rind 1 lemon
grated rind 1 orange
½ cup desiccated coconut.

Method

Mash the tofu and blend with oil and fruit juices.
Add everything else except the coconut and mix well.
If it is too dry, add more fruit juice.
Roll into walnut-sized balls.
Roll in desiccated coconut and refrigerate.

Variations

Other ingredients to try – dried apricots, dried mango, dates.
Your favourite liqueur and glace cherries.
Roll in grated chocolate, or refrigerate and dip in melted chocolate.

These are easy to make, and if you do not have all the ingredients, don't worry – you can simply vary the recipe to suit your pantry or your taste buds.

Pancakes with Blueberry Sauce

Pancake ingredients
1 cup brown rice flour
1 cup white rice flour
1¼ cups water
2 eggs.

Pancake method
Blend everything except the eggs in a food processor.
Allow the mixture to stand for at least two hours.
Then add the eggs and beat.

Brush a frying pan with oil. Pour in some of the mixture.
Cover with a lid and cook on medium-low heat about five
minutes.
Turn with a spatula and cook the other side.

Sauce ingredients
30g butter
¼ cup blueberry jam
2 teaspoons arrowroot
1/3 cup red wine
1 Tbspn brown sugar
1/3 cup gluten-free stock cubes.

Sauce method
Gently melt butter and jam in a saucepan. Add stock, red
wine, sugar and arrowroot keeping it on a low heat, stir until
the sauce thickens.

Serve on pancakes with ice cream.

Apple and Chocolate Muffins
(Makes 8–10 muffins)

Ingredients

½ cup margarine
½ cup sugar
¼ cup cocoa
2 eggs
1½ cups apple puree
½ cup chopped chocolate or chocolate chips
1 cup soy flour
1 cup rice flour
1 tspn baking soda
½ tspn cream of tartar.

Method
Preheat oven to 170°C, prepare pans.
Cream the margarine and sugar then blend in the cocoa.
Beat in the apple puree, chocolate and eggs.
Combine the dry ingredients then carefully mix them into the wet ingredients. Spoon into pans and bake for 30 mins.

Variations
Banana–Chocolate:
Replace the apple puree with 1½ cups mashed bananas.

Coconut and Apple–Chocolate:
Add 1 cup of desiccated coconut to the wet mix.

Fruity Apple–Chocolate:
Add 1 cup of any desired dried fruits to the mixture.

Pikelets

Ingredients
¼ cup maize cornflour
¾ cup rice flour
1 tspn GF baking powder
¼ cup sugar
1 egg
½ cup dairy-free formula or soy milk.

Method
Sift flours and baking powder into a bowl or jug.
Mix in sugar.

Beat egg and formula or soy milk together.
Mix into dry ingredients.

Grease an electric frypan or frying pan with oil or dairy-free margarine.

Cook tablespoon amounts of mixture.

When bubbles start to appear, turn and cook the other side.

Cool on a cooling rack.

Serve with dairy-free margarine.

Apple and Honey Slice

Ingredients
100g margarine
2 Tbspn honey *or* maple syrup *or* corn syrup
1 large or 2 small eggs, beaten
1 cup grated or stewed apple
1½ cups rice flour
1 tspn GF baking powder
1 tspn cinnamon
1 tspn mixed spice
½ tspn nutmeg
1½ cup chopped sultanas
½ cup walnuts (optional and if suitable).

Method
Melt margarine and honey in large saucepan.

Remove from heat and add egg, apple, dried fruit and sifted dry ingredients.

Mix well to combine.

Put in greased sponge roll tin.

Bake for 20–25 mins at 160°C. Cut into fingers or squares.

Natalie's Fruit Balls (no baking required)

Ingredients
2 eggs (beaten)
1 cup sugar
1 cup mixed fruit
2 Tbspn cocoa
100g butter
½ tspn vanilla essence
2 cups flaked rice *or* GF cornflakes
coconut.

Method
Place beaten eggs, sugar, mixed fruit, cocoa and butter in a saucepan.

Cook on low heat for 10 minutes until thick.
Add vanilla and remove from heat.
Allow to cool, then stir in the flaked rice.

Roll teaspoonfuls into balls.

Chill slightly and roll in coconut.

Sultanas or dates may be used instead of mixed fruit.

Lemon Slice (no baking required)

Ingredients

Half a 415g can condensed milk
125g butter, melted
250g GF cornflakes, crushed
    or 250g GF rice cookies, crushed
½ cup desiccated coconut
½ cup shredded coconut
1 Tbspn lemon juice
Grated rind of 1 lemon or mandarin.

Icing

250g pure icing sugar
2 Tbspns butter, melted
2 Tbspns lemon juice
A little hot water.

Method

Mix the slice ingredients well. Press into a lightly greased dish.

In a separate bowl, bash the lumps out of the pure icing sugar. Add 2 Tablespoons of melted butter and 2 Tablespoons of lemon juice. Mix well.

Very slowly add a little hot water until the icing is soft enough. Spread over the slice mixture.

Refrigerate for a few hours. Cut into fingers.

Great Lunch Box
morning or afternoon tea ideas

Food Necklaces

Food necklaces are a great fun way for children to eat a variety of different foods.

Mix the following suggested foods together:

Fresh fruit: slices apricots, kiwifruit, grapes, oranges or mandarins.

Dried fruit: raisins, apples, dates, prunes, apricots, pineapples.

Vegetables: celery, carrots, small tomatoes, mushrooms, radishes, cauliflower, gherkin, pickled onions.

Savoury: cooked GF sausage, walnuts, almonds, cheese, tomato, gherkins.

Use a darning needle and some kitchen string and thread the food on this. Or use bamboo skewers or toothpicks.

Prune Mice

Remove stones from prunes and fill with walnuts, almonds or brazil nuts.

Split an almond in two to make the ears, currants for the eyes and a thin strip of GF liquorice for the tail.

Apple and/or Pear Sandwiches

Ingredients

    1 apple *or* pear
    2 slices cheese
    2 slices ham
    1 Tbspn lemon juice.

Method

Core the apple or pear (with skin on) and slice into rings.
Soak the slices in the lemon juice to stop them from going brown.
Cut the cheese and meat to fit the size of the fruit slices.
Put the cheese and meat between the slices.

Fruit and Cheese balls

Ingredients

    ½ cup cheese
    ¼ cup raisins
    ¼ cup sultanas
    ¼ cup cheese spread
    1/3 cup chopped nuts.

Method

Mix the raisins, sultanas, cheese and spread together.
Shape into 8–10 balls.
Roll in chopped nuts.

Cheese and Bacon Balls

Ingredients

½ cup cream cheese
½ cup walnut halves
2 rashers bacon.

Method
Grill the bacon until crisp, crumble until very fine.
Make the cheese into balls about size of a walnut and press a walnut half on each side. Roll in the crumbled bacon until all of the cheese is coated.

Celery Canoes

Ingredients

Celery stalks
Cottage cheese *or* cheese spread
Raisins
GF Rice bubbles.

Method
Cut the celery into pieces around 5–6 cm long.
Fill in the groove with the cottage cheese.
Press in a few raisins and cover the rest with rice bubbles.

Avocado and Sour Cream Dip

Ingredients

    1 large avocado
    ½ cup cottage cheese
    ¼ cup sour cream
    1 tspn lemon juice
    ½ tspn salt
    few drops of onion juice and Tabasco.

Method
Cut the avocado in half, remove stone, peel and put through sieve. Sieve cottage cheese, then mix avocado, cottage cheese, sour cream, lemon juice and salt together.
Season to taste with onion juice and Tabasco.

School Lunchbox Ideas

A small container with a plastic spoon with some of the following are great ways to fill up tummies at lunchtime.

    Yoghurt – small tub with fresh fruit (home-made).

    GF Jellies with fresh fruit set in (do not use kiwifruit as this won't let the jelly set).

    Pureed fruit with some fresh fruit as well. You can add some dried fruit as well.

Main meals

Spinach and Ricotta Gnocchi

Ingredients

3–4 bunches spinach (24-30 leaves)
250g ricotta cheese
90g parmesan cheese, grated
½ cup GF flour
1 egg
Salt and pepper
¼ tspn nutmeg
1 can (400g) peeled tomatoes.

Method

Wash and dry spinach, remove white stalks. Cook spinach in
a saucepan with the lid on for about 5 minutes. Drain well
and chop finely. Combine the spinach, ricotta cheese, half
the parmesan cheese, the measured GF flour (you may need
more ricotta cheese), egg, salt, pepper and nutmeg in a bowl.
Mix well.

Form mixture into balls, using a tablespoon to mould them.
Roll Gnocchi lightly in GF flour. Bring a large pan of salted
water to the boil and drop gnocchi in, 3 or 4 at a time.
Simmer gently until they rise to the surface, about 1–2
minutes.

Remove from pan with slotted spoon and place in well
greased ovenproof dish.
Place the warmed crushed tomatoes to which you can add
herbs to taste around the gnocchi and sprinkle with remaining
grated parmesan cheese.
Place under moderately hot grill for a few minutes, until
cheese browns.
Serves 2–4.

Vegetable Pakoras

Best eaten as soon as they are cooked. Serves 4–6.

Ingredients

500g assorted vegetable pieces, i.e. cauliflower and broccoli florets, thinly sliced potato, kumara, or pumpkin, small whole mushrooms, slices of peppers, zucchini cut lengthwise.

1½ cups chickpea flour

1 tspn salt

½ tspn chilli powder

1 tspn tumeric

1 tspn ground cumin

1 tspn ground coriander

1 tspn garam masala

1 to 1½ cups water

Vegetable or olive oil to deep fry.

Method

Prepare the vegetables. In a bowl, mix together the dry ingredients. Add half the water, whisk, getting rid of as many lumps as you can. Add the remaining water, plus a little more if necessary, to form a thin coating batter.

Heat oil about 2 cm deep in a suitable pot, deep fryer or electric wok. Dip the vegetable pieces one at a time into the batter to coat them completely, then drop gently into the oil. At first they will sink, but they will rise to the surface again as they cook.

Fry for about 5 minutes or until brown, turning occasionally.

Note: Delicious served with chilli mayonnaise or minted yoghurt for dipping.

Serve with an interesting rice mixture, a tomato salad, and other curry style side dishes if you are entertaining.

Vegetarian Slice

Can be served hot or cold.
Great for school lunches and picnics.

Ingredients

> 1/3 cup melted butter
> 1 250g container cottage cheese
> 5 eggs (beaten)
> 1 onion, chopped
> 1 tspn herbs (e.g. basil, thyme, oreganum, sage)
> 2 Tbspn chopped parsley
> ¼ cup milk
> 200g   GF cornflakes
> 1½ –2 cups cooked, chopped and cooled broccoli
> Salt and pepper.

Method

Beat the eggs in a large bowl then add all the ingredients.

Mix well and press into sponge roll
or into lamington tin approx 24–30 cm.

Bake at 190°C for 40–45 minutes.

Chicken Casserole

Ingredients
    1.5kg (3 lb) chicken pieces
            (for best flavour, leave skin on)
    4 tspns oil
    2 large onions
    4 cloves garlic or crushed garlic
    2 tspns oil, extra
    4 tspns lemon juice
    2 tspns grated lemon rind
    2 cups   GF tomato sauce
    2 tspns brown sugar
    2 tspns GF dry mustard
    2 tspns GF curry powder
    4 tspns GF vinegar
    2 tspns GF soy sauce
    salt and freshly ground pepper.

Method
Sauté chicken in hot oil until golden brown.
Remove from pan, drain.

Pour off oil from pan, add all other ingredients.
Stir until pan brownings are dissolved.
Add chicken.
Cook on low heat until tender.

Nice served with rice and green vegetables.
Freezes well.

Cheese Sauce (without butter)
Ingredients

      1 cup grated cheese
      1 Tbspn maize cornflour
      ½ tspn GF mustard powder
      1 cup milk.

Method

In a plastic bag, toss the cheese, flour and mustard together so that the cornflour coats all the cheese.
Warm the milk in a saucepan.
Add the cheese, stir constantly until the cheese melts and the sauce thickens.

Adjust the desired consistency of the sauce by adding or reducing milk.

You can use this sauce over vegetables, pasta, fish or chicken.

Cheese Sauce (with butter)
Ingredients

      60g butter
      3 level Tbspns maize cornflour
      500ml skim milk
      1 Tbspn parmesan
      60g grated tasty cheese.

Method

Melt butter in a pot.
Add cornflour, stir well. Add skim milk.
Stir constantly until thickened.
Add cheeses. Stir until cheese has melted.

Savoury Rice Bake

Ingredients

    5 cups cooked rice
    4 eggs, beaten
    500g cottage cheese
    250g mushrooms chopped
    2 large chopped onions
    4 or 5 medium size tomatoes, chopped
    2 cups tasty grated cheese
    2 Tbspns sharp parmesan
    6 rashers bacon, chopped
    250g frozen corn kernels
    3 medium tomatoes, sliced
    ¼ tspn salt
    freshly ground black pepper.

Method

Mix everything (except for 1 cup of the grated cheese and the sliced tomatoes) well.

Turn into a greased oven-proof dish 36 x 26cm. Using a smaller, deeper dish is fine – takes a little longer to cook.

Cover the top with slices of tomato and then 1 cup of grated tasty cheese.

Bake at 220°C for about 50 minutes until firm and cooked through.

Serve with green vegetables or salad.   Serves 8–10.

Baked Potatoes

For each person, scrub one large potato and pierce it several times. If you don't, it may explode in the microwave.

Microwave on high for 4–5 minutes: prod it with your finger to check that it is soft.
Cut a deep star across the top, and press from the bottom to open up the potato.

Make any of the following mixtures. Use a food processor to chop the onions, peppers, garlic etc. Pile the mixture in and on top of the potato. Microwave for another one and a half minutes.

Choose any of these fillings
a) Baked beans (gluten-free ones), onion, cheese, and lots of freshly ground pepper.
b) Bacon, onion and cheese.
c) Cooked mince, onion and gluten-free taco mix, mint or parsley.
d) Creamed corn, cheese, onion, chopped chives and freshly ground pepper.
e) Salmon or tuna, onion and chives.
f) Prawns, garlic and a light cheese sauce (made with mild cheese).
g) Bought or home-made pesto.

Optional extras
As well, finely chopped tomatoes, finely chopped celery and capsicum (bell peppers) are all really nice added to any of these mixtures.

Cheesy Potato and Ham Casserole

Ingredients

    3 medium potatoes, peeled and thinly sliced
    1 onion, sliced
    2 hard-boiled eggs, chopped
    ¾ cup grated tasty cheese
    ¼ cup cooked ham, chopped
    ½ cup milk
    2 Tbspn GF chutney
    ¼ tspn paprika
    freshly ground black pepper
    herb salt.

Method

Grease an oven-proof dish with half the potato and onion slices. Sprinkle with salt and pepper.

Spread the cheese, ham, chutney and eggs over the potato slices.

Pour the milk over it. Use the remaining potato and onion slices to make another layer.

Add the milk and sprinkle with paprika.

Bake at 180°C in oven for about 30 minutes. By then, the potatoes should be tender.

Kumara and Corn Casserole

You can use pumpkin instead, if you like.

Ingredients

      1 large or several small kumara
      440g corn kernels, fresh, frozen or canned (drained)
      2 cups GF cornflakes
      ½ cup chopped onion
      ½ cup chopped green and red capsicum
      2 Tbspns margarine
      1 cup grated low-fat tasty cheese
      ¼ cup sharp parmesan, grated
      a few pieces of lemon grass
      salt and freshly ground pepper to taste.

Method

Boil the sweet potatoes in water containing lemon grass. When they're soft, fish out the lemon grass and throw it away. Mash the sweet potatoes. You need two cups of mashed sweet potato.

Gently cook onions, capsicums and 2 tablespoons of margarine in a medium saucepan. Do not brown.
Stir in corn and sweet potato and half the cornflakes.
Blend all together and put in greased casserole dish.

Sprinkle over the top in this order: remaining cornflakes, parmesan cheese and grated tasty cheese.

Bake uncovered in a 180°C oven for about 45 minutes until nicely browned on top.

Serves 6.

Stuffed Capsicums

These are easy to make and taste great.
Make sure the stock cubes and sauce are gluten-free.

Ingredients

> 5 large capsicums (bell peppers)
> 1 cup long grain rice
> 2 GF beef stock cubes
> 250g mince
> 750g your favourite GF pasta sauce
> 1 cup tasty cheese, grated
> ¼ cup extra sharp parmesan.

Method

Boil or microwave rice in water to which you have added the beef stock cubes. Mix mince and half the pasta sauce. Microwave on high for about 10 minutes (or cook in frypan).

If possible select squarish capsicums which will stand on end. Remove the seeds and stringy pieces.
Add the cooked rice to the cooked mince.
Add 1 cupful grated cheese.
Mix well and spoon mixture into capsicums.

Stand capsicums in a microwave dish, pour remaining pasta sauce over them, top with parmesan cheese, cover and cook on high for about 15 minutes, *or* bake in oven for about half an hour at 180°C.

Variation: If you are rushed for time, don't stuff the capsicums, just slice them and mix everything together.

Fast Beef Stroganoff (microwave)

Ingredients
      500g beef mince (ground beef)
      1 packet GF onion soup mix
      3 cups   GF rice noodles
      ½ tspn ground ginger
      3½ cups hot water
      1 can sliced mushrooms
      1 cup cream
      maize cornflour.

Method
Microwave mince on high for 5 minutes.

Add packet of soup, noodles, ginger, hot water.

Cook for 12 minutes.

Add mushrooms and cream and thicken with maize cornflour.

Microwave for another minute.

Bacon, Potato and Onion Pie

Ingredients

2 large potatoes, thinly sliced
2 large onions, sliced
6 rashers of bacon
2 eggs
pepper and herb salt
1 cup milk.

Method

Place layers in a greased oven-proof dish in this order: onion, bacon, potato.

Repeat.
Top layer should be potato.

Beat two eggs, add seasoning.

Add milk and pour over the layers.

Bake in oven at 190°C until the top browns.

Salmon and Potato Bake

Ingredients

440g   tinned salmon
500g   potatoes, boiled and sliced
60g   butter
3 Tbspns GF flour
1½ cups milk
3 Tbspns maize cornflour
½ cup cream
1 small onion, finely chopped
1 tspn GF dry mustard
½ cup tasty cheese, grated
½ cup GF cornflakes
½ teaspoon paprika.

Method

Melt the butter in a saucepan, add the flour and cook for one minute. Add the cream and milk and gently bring to the boil, stirring constantly until the sauce thickens.

Remove from stove and add the mustard, half the cheese and gently fold in the salmon.
Avoid mashing it.

In an oven-proof dish, arrange alternative layers of potato slices and the salmon mixture.
Sprinkle cornflakes over the top, followed by the remaining cheese and paprika.

Bake in 180°C oven for about half an hour until nicely golden brown on top.

Serve with green vegetables or salad.

Rice Tomato Pilaf

Ingredients

30g   butter
2 cups   white rice
½ cup   wild rice
3 cups   tomato juice
1 tspn   salt
½ tspn   freshly ground black pepper
1 tspn   cumin
2 bay   leaves
1 tspn   coriander.

Method

Bring water to boil, add rice and wild rice.

Add everything else.

Simmer gently until all the water is absorbed – about 15 minutes.

Cover and let it stand a few minutes.

Serve with salad and cold meat.

Potato and Vegetable Wedges

Here is a tasty way to cook veges.

Ingredients

  3 potatoes
  1 large kumara
  1 parsnip
  3 carrots
  1 Tbspn oil
  1 tspn paprika
  1 tspn GF curry powder
  ½ tspn freshly ground black pepper.

Method

Scrub the vegetables and cut them into wedges.
Toss them in oil in a large oven-proof dish.

Mix the paprika, curry powder and pepper and sprinkle it
over the wedges.

Stir well to make sure the pieces are covered.
Bake at 200°C for 20–30 minutes until the wedges are
delightfully golden brown and crunchy.

Turn them over a couple of times during baking.

Home-made Fish and Chips

To enjoy fish and chips, either make a tempura batter using maize cornflour instead of flour, or coat the fish with GF Pancake, Waffle and Pikelet mix. Then dip into beaten egg, and then coat with crushed GF cornflakes.

To make oven-bake low-fat chips use 6 large potatoes and cut into chips or wedges. Pat dry on a paper towel.

In a large bowl mix:
> ½ cup white rice flour
> 4 Tbspn cooking oil
> 1 Tbspn GF soy sauce
> ½ tspn spices of your choice (optional)
>> e.g. cumin, coriander and mixed spice.

Stir the wedges in a bowl to coat them.

Place on oven trays in single layers and bake at 210°C for 30 minutes (fan bake if available).

Turning the chips over after 15 minutes will help prevent them from sticking.

 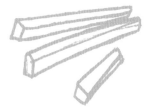

Gluten-free recipes for you – Free

We would like to give you some recipes.
These are free for you. Just go to the website

www.doctorgluten.com

All you have to do is put in your user name and
password. Then you can get your free recipes
and much more information.

Go to **www.doctorgluten.com**

Your User name: **gluten**
Your Password: **free**

Then you can get your free recipes

Other books by Doctor Rodney Ford

The Energy Effect? Your Questions Answered

Dr Rodney Ford, nutritional and energy expert, teaches
you how to live each day with High Energy. He shows
you how to use the combination of your body, brain and
concsiousness to create "The Energy Effect". Do you
find that you lack time or energy to do all that you want?
Do you want feel energized so you can keep on going –
and going – to the end of your day? The Energy Effect
gives you complete answers on how you can create
more energy in your life. (192 pages)

ISBN-10: 0-473-10259-5

ISBN-13: 978-0-473-10259-3 (NZ$34.95 Aus$34.95 US$19.95)

Other books by DoctorGluten

These three books have been written for you to give you all the help and advice you will need to master the gluten-free diet.

Going Gluten-Free: How to Get Started

"Overwhelm" is the first emotion felt when you are confronted by the prospect of a gluten-free diet. So, find out how you can easily get started. Step1– Get ready: Check out your symptoms and blood tests. Step 2 – Get set up: find out all about gluten. Use our shopping list. Learn what you can eat and what to avoid. Step 3 – Go gluten-free: follow the recipes and eating ideas. Gluten-free can be a great experience.(64 pages)

ISBN-10: 0-473-10491-1

ISBN-13: 978-0-473-10491-7   (NZ$14.95 Aus$14.95 US$9.95)

The Gluten-free Lunch Book

What can I have for lunch? This is our most often asked question. Easy and yummy lunches make all the difference if you are trying to stay gluten-free. We have brought together the best lunch ideas so you never have to worry about lunch again. Simple and delicious gluten-free lunch box ideas for you and your family. Follow these recipes and eating ideas for a great gluten-free experience. (64 pages)

ISBN-10: 0-473-10498-9

ISBN-13: 978-0-473-10498-6   (NZ$14.95 Aus$14.95 US$9.95)

Gluten-free Parties and Picnics

Oh dear, it's Libby's birthday. So how will we manage to do a gluten-free party? And what will we do when we go on a family picnic? These are common questions that are answered for your children in a story-book format, in full colour. It is packed full of ideas for a great party and fun picnics. Also great for educating your family and friends about gluten-free issues. These family stories make the gluten-free issues easy for your children to learn and understand. There are heaps of useful ideas for fun and simple gluten-free eating. (64 pages full colour)

ISBN-10: 0-473-10774-0

ISBN-13: 978-0-473-10774-1   (NZ$19.95 Aus$19.95 US$14.95)

These books give you much more in-depth information about gluten prblems and how it can adversely affect you and your family. It answers the hundreds of questions you will have.

Are You Gluten-Sensitive? Your Questions Answered

This book is based on the questions that I am repeatedly asked by my patients. I answer their questions in detail and put them into the clinical context. There is so much confusion about the diagnosis and management of people who are gluten-sensitive. This book has been written to clarify this muddle. It is full of practical information. You can work out if you are affected by gluten. One in ten people react to gluten – you could be that one. Right now is a good time to find out. (192 pages)
ISBN-10: 0-473-11229-9
ISBN-13: 978-0-473-11229-5 (NZ$34.95 Aus$34.95 US$19.95)

The book for the Sick, Tired & Grumpy (Gluten-free kids)

Fifty people tell their amazing gluten stories. A cure for people who feel sick, tired or grumpy. These personal accounts are very moving with a raw honesty. If you want to feel well and full of energy again – then this book is for you. These children and parents tell about their low energy, their irritability and their troublesome symptoms before they discovered their gluten-sensitivity. Going gluten-free has changed their lives – a miracle cure! This might be just the answer for you. (192 pages)
ISBN-10: 0-473-11228-0
ISBN-13: 978-0-473-11228-8 (NZ$34.95 Aus$34.95 US$19.95)

Full of it! The shocking truth about gluten

Alarmingly, gluten can damage your brain. Have you ever wondered why you crave for another hunk of bread? If a food that you ate was slowly eroding the ability of your brain, then would you want to know what that food was? It might be gluten! Gluten is linked to ataxia, migraine, ADHD, autism, depression, epilepsy, mood and psychiatric disorders. Gluten also can disrupt the brain's regulation of your gut – this can cause mayhem in your bowel. This book give the evidence that gluten-sensitivity is a brain disease! Read the evidence for yourself. (192 pages)
ISBN-10: 0-473-10407-5
ISBN-13: 978-0-473-10407-8 (NZ$34.95 Aus$34.95 US$19.95)

All books available from our website: www.doctorgluten.com

❏ **Going Gluten-Free: How to Get Started**
❏ **The Gluten-Free Lunch Book**
❏ **Gluten-Free Parties and Picnics**
❏ **Are You Gluten-Sensitive? Your Questions Answered**
❏ The book for the **Sick, Tired & Grumpy**
❏ **Full Of It! The shocking truth about gluten**
❏ **The Energy Effect? Your Questions Answered**

(Please indicate the number of each book that you want to order. Prices stated on previous pages)
Please add postage & handling: 1 book $7.00, 2 books $12, 3 or 4 books $15

(Prices for postage and handling to be paid in the currency of purchase)

Order for:

Date of order: _____ / _____ / _____

Name: _____

Postal address: _____

_____

Phone: _____ Fax: _____

Email: _____ @ _____

Number of books required: _____ Currency _____

Cost of books $ _____ Postage $ _____ Total $_____

Method of payment:

Cheque ❏   Visa ❏   MasterCard ❏   (please tick)

Cardholder's name: _____

Credit card number : _____

Signature: _____ Expiry date: _____ / _____

Please make your cheque payable to:
Doctor Gluten, PO Box 25-360, Christchurch, New Zealand.
Fax orders: +64 3 377 3605
Phone: +64 3 377 3602
Email orders: orders@doctorgluten.com
Web orders: www.doctorgluten.com
(Please allow up to 21 days for postal delivery)